FREEDOM

Take and Receive series

FREEDOM

A Guide for Prayer

by
Jacqueline Syrup Bergan
S. Marie Schwan

Take and Receive series

Saint Mary's Press
Christian Brothers Publications
Winona, Minnesota

Dedicated to
the Spirit of the Risen Christ
alive in our world

 Genuine recycled paper with 10% post-consumer waste.
Printed with soy-based ink.

Companion books are available in this Take and Receive
series. Write to
Saint Mary's Press
702 Terrace Heights
Winona, MN 55987-1320

All Unless noted otherwise below, all scriptural excerpts
are from *The New Jerusalem Bible.* Copyright © 1985, by
Darton, Longman & Todd, Limited, and Doubleday Publishing & Group. Used with permission of the publisher.

The scriptural quote on page 61 is from *The Jerusalem Bible.*
Copyright © 1966 by Darton, Longman & Todd, Limited
and Doubleday & Company, Inc. Used with permission of
the publisher.

The scriptural excerpts on pages 89 and 93 are from the
Revised Standard Version of the Bible, copyright © 1946,
1952, 1971 by the Division of Christian Education of the
National Council of the Churches of Christ of the U.S.A.

The acknowledgments continue on pages x and 161.

Printed in the United States of America

Printing: 12 11 10 9

Year 2001

ISBN 0-88489-172-0

Contents

Do You Love Me? Do You Love Me? Do You Love Me? (John 21:15,17)
Week 5

Receive the Holy Spirit (John 20:22)
Week 6

You Will Be My Witnesses to the Ends of the Earth (Acts 1:8)

Foreword

We escaped like a bird
from the fowlers' net.
The net was broken
and we escaped.
> (Ps. 124:7)

Just as a bird is meant to fly with full freedom and to fill the heavens with its song of joy, so we—through the resurrection and ascension of Jesus and through the gift of the Holy Spirit—are meant to be free and to sing a new song of joy.

We "were called to be free; do not use your freedom as an opening for self-indulgence, but be servants to one another in love" (Gal. 5:13). It is a freedom that gives free rein to the Spirit of God within us, and this leads to joy and peace (Gal. 5:22).

Very few people are fully free; something binds most of us; something imprisons most of us. To the extent that we are not free, our song of Christian joy is muted, maybe even silenced.

This fifth and final volume in the Take and Receive series emphasizes the freedom and joy that ought to be ours in the Risen Christ through the Spirit of God. May this volume enable us all to experience this freedom and to express it with joy and peace wherever we are, even in the midst of ugliness, corruption, and destruction. Then we will be a sign of resurrection and life and hope to those who need it most.

†Victor H. Balke
Bishop of Crookston
Crookston, Minnesota

Ascension Thursday, 1987

Acknowledgments

In concluding the five volumes of the Take and Receive series, our hearts are filled with gratitude to all the people who have supported and encouraged us during the years of this endeavor.

We wish to thank our families and friends, especially Leonard, Jackie's husband, for his sustaining presence of love to her; the sisters of Saint Joseph, Marie's community, for their confidence and caring; Rev. Dick Rice, SJ, for his willingness to critique each manuscript; S. M. Christine Johnson, our typist, for persevering through all five volumes; to our publishers, Saint Mary's Press, whose vision is making possible the outreach of this work; our bishop, Victor Balke, for his belief and trust; the individuals who have participated, over the years, in our days of prayer; and the many readers who have written letters of gratitude and encouragement to us.

We also wish to offer gratitude to each other for the particular gifts each brought to the work, as well as for the continuing vulnerability and faithfulness that such a collaboration calls for.

Most of all, we are grateful to God for the inspiration and sustaining grace that brought this work to completion.

Now, we surrender our efforts to God.

"Take, Lord, and receive" (43, p. 141).

Cover Design

SONG OF SONGS 2:11–12

"For see, winter is past,
the rains are over and gone.

"Flowers are appearing on the earth.
The season of glad songs has come,
the cooing of the turtledove is heard
in our land."

A "season of glad songs" has begun; throughout the Church is heard the murmur of prayer. Quietly, and in stillness, within the hearts of Christians everywhere, winter has given way to the vitality of spring—the coming of the Spirit.

Among the heralds of spring is the return and nesting of birds. From the days of ancient Israel even to our own times, birds have been symbolic, not only of our deep homing instincts but also of our creative impulse and of our desire for transcendence.

Frequent allusions to doves are made throughout the Scriptures. In Song of Songs, the dove announces spring; in Genesis, the olive-bearing dove indicates the end of the flood (Gen. 8:11). At the baptism of Jesus, the Holy Spirit descends on Jesus in the form of a dove (Mark 1:10).

The pair of doves on the cover of volume one of the Take and Receive series, *Love,* symbolizes God's call to love. The cover of volume two, *Forgiveness,* depicts the blessing and nurturing of God's unconditional and forgiving love. The cover of volume three, *Birth,* represents the creative Spirit of God hovering over our world, birthing new life. The empty nest on the cover of volume four, *Surrender,* symbolically conveys the self-emptying love to which Christ submitted himself, in life and death, and to which we as his followers are called. The four doves on the cover of volume five, *Freedom,* represent the Easter community formed in the power and peace of the Risen Christ who is actively present in our world. The use of the specific number of four doves connotes wholeness and totality: the four cardinal points of creation, the four seasons, the winds, the sides of a square, the arms of the cross. The doves suggest the integration of the four functions of the human personality: intuition and sensation, feeling and thinking.

The mourning dove calls: "'Come then, my beloved. / For see, winter is past'" (Song of Songs 2:10–11).

The covers were designed by Donna Pierce Campbell, a popular Minnesota artist whose freshness of style mirrors the spirit of renewal that this guide for prayer hopes to serve.

Introduction

This guide for prayer was inspired by the spiritual hunger we witnessed during the past years as we conducted parish days of renewal throughout northwestern Minnesota.

People shared with us their need and eagerness for guidance and support in developing a personal relationship with God. Gradually we grew in the awareness that for too long the laity has been deprived of resources that are an integral part of the tradition of spirituality within the Church.

One treasure within this tradition is the Spiritual Exercises of Saint Ignatius. The Exercises were a response to the need of the laity in the sixteenth century and have only recently been discovered anew. In the light of Vatican Council II, with its emphasis on the Scriptures, interior renewal, and the emergence of the laity, the Exercises have received a new relevance.

As we endeavored to adapt the pattern of the Exercises to parish days of renewal, we discovered an approach for integrating personal prayer with life circumstances that is appropriate to the needs, language, and lifestyle of the laity.

Freedom: A Guide for Prayer is the fifth of five volumes in the Take and Receive series; each book provides a series of scriptural passages with commentaries and suggested approaches to prayer. The theme of each volume directly correlates with a segment of the Exercises, though each book can be used independently of the others.

The first book in the series, *Love,* makes use of the themes present in the "Principle and Foundation" of the Spiritual Exercises. These themes are the affirmation of human creaturehood, indifference to all created things, and commitment. The guide centers on God's love, our total dependence on that love, and the call to respond in freedom to praise, reverence, and serve God.

The second volume, *Forgiveness,* correlates with the first week of the Spiritual Exercises of Saint Ignatius. The themes treat personal and collective sinfulness insofar as it is an obstacle to receiving God's love. Sin and sinner are considered in light of God's merciful and forgiving love.

Volume three, *Birth,* leads the reader toward a personal discovery of the profound significance of the life of Christ as the paradigm of each person's passage into a way of living that incarnates the Spirit of Jesus in our world. We are invited to contemplate the earthly life of Jesus from his incarnation to and throughout his public ministry.

Volume four, *Surrender*, focuses on Christ's total submission to the will of God. Through the contemplation of Jesus' passion and death, his followers are led to an awareness of how suffering can be used and transformed.

In volume five, *Freedom*, we contemplate Christ in his resurrection appearances to those he loved, to those who believed in and followed him. Gently we are drawn, through prayer, into an experience of the joy and presence of the Spirit of the Risen Christ dwelling within us, inviting us to share his vision and mission. Through our collaboration with his Spirit in creating the New Age, the power and healing energy of God is dynamically released into today's world.

Written specifically as a support for solitary prayer, the guides can also serve as a resource for faith-sharing in small groups and as a program of renewal for parishes and congregations.

The series of guides makes no claim to be the Spiritual Exercises nor to be a commentary on them. The series attempts to make available a means of entering into the Christocentric dynamic of conversion found in the Exercises.

In writing this approach to prayer, we hope that more people will be able to draw nourishment from the word of God, experience God's unique love for them, and become aware of the particular intention God holds for each of them.

Although we have attempted to be sensitive to the use of inclusive language in the commentaries and approaches to prayer, we have not been entirely consistent. In some instances we have been reluctant to make changes in the biblical text out of respect for the word of God and for those people who may find such changes offensive.

Our prayer for those who use this guide is that they will be led by the Spirit of Christ into true spiritual freedom.

May the God of our Lord Jesus Christ, the Father of glory, give you a spirit of wisdom and perception of what is revealed, to bring you to full knowledge of him. May he enlighten the eyes of your mind so that you can see what hope his call holds for you, how rich is the glory of the heritage he offers among his holy people, and how extraordinarily great is the power that he has exercised for us believers. (Eph. 1:17–19)

Jacqueline Syrup Bergan
S. Marie Schwan

7 June 1987
Feast of Pentecost

Orientations

LUKE 11:1

Lord, teach us to pray.

Prayer is our personal response to God's presence. We approach the Lord reverently with a listening heart. God speaks first. In prayer, we acknowledge the Divine presence and in gratitude respond to God in love. The focus is always on God and on what God does.

The following suggestions are offered as ways of supporting and enabling attentiveness to God's word and awareness of our unique response.

A. DAILY PATTERN OF PRAYER

For each period of prayer, use the following pattern:

1. Preparation
- Plan to spend at least twenty minutes to one hour in prayer daily. Though there is nothing sacred about sixty minutes, most people find that an hour better provides for the quieting of self, the entrance into the passage, and so on.
- The evening before, take time to read the commentary as well as the scriptural passage for the following day. Just before falling asleep, recall the scriptural passage.

2. Structure of the Prayer Period
- Quiet yourself; be still inside and out. Relax. Breathe in deeply, hold your breath to the count of four, then exhale slowly through your mouth. Repeat several times.
- Realize you are nothing without God; declare your dependency.
- Ask God for the grace you want and need.
- Read and reflect on your chosen scriptural passage, using the appropriate form; for example, use meditation for poetic and nonstory passages, contemplation for story-event passages, and so on. See "Forms of Solitary Prayer," page 2.

1

- Close the prayer period with a time of conversation with Jesus and his Father. Speak and listen. Conclude with an Our Father.

3. Review of Prayer

The review of prayer is a reflection at the conclusion of the prayer period. The purpose of the review is to heighten our awareness of how God has been present to us during the prayer period.

The review focuses primarily on the interior movements of consolation and desolation as they are revealed in our feelings of joy, peace, sadness, fear, ambivalence, anger. Often it is in the review that we become aware of how God has responded to our request for a particular grace.

Writing the review provides for personal accountability and is a precious record of our spiritual journey. To write the review is a step toward self-integration. In the absence of a spiritual director or a spiritual companion, the writing helps fill the need for evaluation and clarification. If one has a spiritual director, the written review offers an excellent means of preparing to share one's prayer experience.

Method: In a notebook or journal, after each prayer period, indicate the date and the passage. Answer each of the following questions:
- Did any word or phrase particularly strike you?
- What were your feelings? Were you peaceful? loving? trusting? sad? discouraged? What do these feelings say to you?
- How are you more aware of God's presence?
- Would returning to some point be helpful in your next prayer period?

B. FORMS OF SOLITARY PRAYER

Scriptural prayer has various forms, and different forms appeal to different people. Eventually, by trying various methods, we become adept at using approaches that are appropriate to particular passages and are in harmony with our personality and needs.

This guide will make use of the following forms:

2

1. Meditation

In meditation we approach the scriptural passage like a love letter; this approach is especially helpful in praying poetic passages.

Method:
- Read the passage slowly, aloud or in a whisper, letting the words wash over you and savoring them.
- Stay with the words that especially catch your attention; absorb them the way the thirsty earth receives the rain.
- Keep repeating a word or phrase, aware of the feelings that are awakened.
- Read and reread the passage lovingly as you would a letter from a dear friend, or as you would softly sing the chorus of a song.

2. Contemplation

In contemplation, we enter into a life event or story passage of the Scriptures by way of imagination, making use of all our senses.

Theologians tell us that through contemplation we are able to "recall and be present at the mysteries of Christ's life" (38, p. 149).

The Spirit of Jesus, present within us through baptism, teaches us, just as Jesus taught the Apostles. The Spirit recalls and enlivens the particular mystery into which we enter through prayer. Just as in the Eucharist the Risen Jesus makes present the paschal mystery, in contemplation he brings forward the particular event we are contemplating and presents himself within that mystery.

Method: In contemplation, we enter the story as if we were there.
- Watch what happens; listen to what is being said.
- Become part of the mystery; assume the role of one of the persons.
- Look at each of the individuals; what does he or she experience? To whom does each one speak?
- What difference does it make for my life, my family, for society, if I hear the message?

In the gospel stories, enter into dialogue with Jesus.
- Be there with him and for him.

- Want him; hunger for him.
- Listen to him.
- Let him be for you what he wants to be.
- Respond to him (109, pp. 5–6).

3. Centering Prayer

"In centering prayer we go beyond thought and image, beyond the senses and the rational mind to that center of our being where God is working a wonderful work" (86, p. 28).

Centering prayer is a very simple, pure form of prayer, frequently without words; it is an opening of our hearts to the Spirit dwelling within us.

In centering prayer, we spiral down into the deepest center of ourselves. It is the point of stillness within us where we most experience being created by a loving God who is breathing us into life. To enter into centering prayer requires a recognition of our dependency on God and a surrender to God's Spirit of love.

"The Spirit too comes to help us in our weakness . . . the Spirit . . . makes our petitions for us in groans that cannot be put into words" (Rom. 8:26).

The Spirit of Jesus within us cries out "'Abba, Father!'" (Rom. 8:15).

Method: "'Be still and acknowledge that I am God'" (Ps. 46:10).
- Sit quietly, comfortable and relaxed.
- Rest within your longing and desire for God.
- Move to the center within your deepest self. To facilitate this movement, form an image of yourself slowly descending in an elevator, or walking down flights of stairs, or descending a mountain, or going down into the water, as in a deep pool.
- In the stillness, become aware of God's presence; peacefully absorb God's love.

4. Mantra

One means of centering prayer is the use of the mantra, or prayer word. The mantra can be a single word or a phrase. It may be a word from the Scriptures or one that arises spontaneously from within your heart. The word or phrase represents, for you, the fullness of God.

4

Variations of the mantra may include the name "Jesus" or what is known as the Jesus prayer, "Lord, Jesus Christ, Son of the Living God, have mercy on me, a sinner."

Method: Repeat the word or phrase slowly within yourself in harmony with your breathing. For example, say the first part of the Jesus prayer while inhaling; say the second half while exhaling.

5. Meditative Reading

"I opened my mouth; he gave me the scroll to eat and then said, '. . . feed on this scroll which I am giving you and eat your fill.' So I ate it, and it tasted sweet as honey" (Ezek. 3:2–3).

One cf the approaches to prayer is a reflective reading of the Scriptures or other spiritual writings.

Spiritual reading is always enriching to our life of prayer. The method described below is especially supportive in times when prayer is difficult or dry.

Method: Read slowly, pausing periodically to allow the words and phrases to enter into you. When a thought resonates deeply, stay with it, allowing the fullness of it to penetrate your being. Relish the word received. Respond authentically and spontaneously, as in a dialogue.

6. Journaling

"A reading of [my words] will enable you to perceive my understanding of the mystery of Christ" (Eph. 3:4).

Journaling is meditative writing. When we place pen on paper, spirit and body cooperate to release our true selves.

There is a difference between journaling and keeping a journal.

To journal is to experience ourselves in a new light as expression is given to the fresh images that emerge from our subconscious. Journaling requires putting aside preconceived ideas and control.

Meditative writing is like writing a letter to one we love. We recall memories, clarify convictions, and our affections well up within us. In writing we may discover that emotions are intensified and prolonged.

5

Because of this, journaling can also serve in identifying and healing hidden, suppressed emotions such as anger, fear, and resentment.

Finally, journaling can give us a deeper appreciation for the written word as we encounter it in the Scriptures.

Method: Among the many variations of journaling in prayer are the following:
- writing a letter addressed to God
- writing a conversation between oneself and another (The other may be Jesus or another significant person. The dialogue can also be with an event, an experience, or a value. For example, death, separation, or wisdom receives personal attributes and is imagined as a person with whom one enters into conversation.)
- writing an answer to a question, such as, "'What do you want me to do for you?'" (Mark 10:51), or "'Why are you weeping?'" (John 20:15)
- allowing Jesus or another scriptural person to speak to us through the pen

7. Repetition

"I will remain quietly meditating upon the point in which I have found what I desire without any eagerness to go on till I have been satisfied" (Saint Ignatius of Loyola (109, p. 110).

Repetition is the return to a previous period of prayer for the purpose of allowing the movements of God to deepen within our heart.

Through repetitions, we fine-tune our sensitivities to God and to how God speaks in our prayer and within our life circumstances. The prayer of repetition allows for the experience of integrating who we are with who God is revealing himself to be for us.

Repetition is a way of honoring God's word to us in the earlier prayer period. It is recalling and pondering an earlier conversation with one we love. It is as if we say to God, "Tell me that again; what did I hear you saying?"

In this follow-up conversation, or repetition, we open ourselves to a healing presence that often transforms whatever sadness and confusion we may have experienced in the first prayer.

In repetitions, not only is our consolation (joy, warmth, peace) deepened, but our desolation (pain, sadness, confusion) is frequently better understood and accepted within God's plan for us.

Method: The period of prayer that we select to repeat is one in which we have experienced a significant movement of joy or sadness or confusion. It may also be a period in which nothing seemed to happen, due, perhaps, to our own lack of readiness at the time.

- Recall the feelings of the first period of prayer.
- As a point of entry, use the scene, word, or feeling that was previously most significant.
- Allow the Spirit to direct the inner movements of your heart during this time of prayer.

C. SPIRITUAL PRACTICES AND HELPS

1. Examen of Consciousness

"Yahweh, you examine me and know me" (Ps. 139:1).

The examen of consciousness is the instrument by which we discover how God has been present to us and how we have responded to that presence through the day.

Saint Ignatius believed this practice was so important that, in the event it was impossible to have a formal prayer period, he insisted that the examen would sustain one's vital link with God.

The examen of consciousness is not to be confused with an examination of conscience in which penitents are concerned with their failures. It is, rather, an exploration of how God is present within the events, circumstances, feelings of our daily life.

What the review is to the prayer period, the examen is to our daily life. The daily discipline of an authentic practice of the examen effects the integrating balance that is essential for growth in relationship to God, to self, and to others.

The method reflects the "dynamic movement of personal love: what we always want to say to a person whom we truly love in the order in which we want

7

to say it. . . . Thank you. . . . Help me. . . . I love you. . . . I'm sorry. . . . Be with me" (31, pp. 34–35).

Method: The following prayer is a suggested approach to examen. You can incorporate the written responses into the prayer journal.

- God, my Creator, I am totally dependent on you. Everything is a gift from you. *All is gift.* I give you thanks and praise for the gifts of this day. . . .
- Lord, I believe you work through and in time to reveal me to myself. Please give me an increased awareness of how you are guiding and shaping my life, as well as a more sensitive awareness of the obstacles I put in your way.
- You have been present in my life today. Be near, now, as I reflect on these things:

  your presence in the *events* of today . . .

  your presence in the *feelings* I experienced today . . .

  your *call* to me . . .

  my *response* to you . . .
- God, I ask your loving forgiveness and healing. The particular event of this day that I most want healed is . . .
- Filled with hope and a firm belief in your love and power, I entrust myself to your care and strongly affirm . . . (Claim the gift that you most desire, most need; believe that God desires to give you that gift.)

2. Faith-sharing

"'For where two or three meet in my name, I am there among them'" (Matt. 18:20).

In the creation of community, members must communicate intimately with each other about the core issues of their lives. For the Christian, this is faith-sharing and is an extension of daily, solitary prayer.

A faith-sharing group is not a discussion group, not a sensitivity session or a social gathering. Members do not come together to share and receive intellectual or theological insights. Nor is the purpose of faith-sharing the accomplishment of some predetermined task.

The purpose of faith-sharing is to listen and to be open to God, who continues to be revealed in the church community represented in the small group that comes together in God's name. The fruit of faith-sharing is the building up of the Church, the Body of Christ (Eph. 4:12).

The approach to faith-sharing is one of reading and reflecting together on the word of God. Faith-sharing calls us to share with each other, out of our deepest center, what it means to be a follower of Christ in our world today. To authentically enter into faith-sharing is to come to know and love each other in Christ, whose Spirit is the bonding force of community.

An image that faith-sharing groups may find helpful is that of a pool into which pebbles are dropped. The group members gather in a circle and imagine themselves around a pool. Like a pebble being gently dropped into the water, each one offers a reflection—his or her "word" from God. In the shared silence, each offering is received. As the water ripples in concentric circles toward the outer reaches of the pool, so too this word enlarges and embraces, in love, each member of the circle.

Method: A group of seven to ten members gathers at a prearranged time and place.

- The leader calls the group to prayer and invites members to some moments of silent centering, during which they pray for the presence of the Holy Spirit.
- The leader gathers their silent prayer in an opening prayer, spontaneous or prepared.
- One of the members reads a previously chosen scriptural passage on which participants have spent some time in solitary prayer.
- A period of silence follows each reading of the Scriptures.
- The leader invites each one to share a word or phrase from the reading.
- Another member rereads the passage; this is followed by a time of silence.
- The leader invites those who wish to share how this passage personally addresses them, for example, by challenging, comforting, inviting.
- Again the passage is read.
- Members are invited to offer their spontaneous prayer to the Lord.

- The leader ends the time of faith-sharing with a prayer, a blessing, an Our Father, or a hymn.
- Before the group disbands, the passage for the following session is announced.

3. The Role of Imagination in Prayer

Imagination is our power of memory and recall that enables us to enter into the experience of the past and to create the future. Through images we are able to touch the center of who we are and bring to the surface and give life and expression to the innermost levels of our being.

The use of images is important to our psycho-spiritual development. Images simultaneously reveal multiple levels of meaning and are therefore symbolic of our deeper reality.

Through the structured use of active imagination, we release the hidden energy and potential for wholeness that is already present within us.

When we use active imagination in the context of prayer, and with an attitude of faith, we open ourselves to the power and mystery of God's transforming presence within us.

Because the Scriptures are, for the most part, a collection of stories and rich in sensual imagery, the use of active imagination in praying the Scriptures is particularly enriching. Through using imagination in praying the Scriptures we go beyond the truth of history to discover the truth of the mystery of God's creative word in our life (36, p. 76).

4. Coping with Distractions

Do not become overly concerned or discouraged by distractions during prayer. Simply put them aside and return to your prayer material. If and when a distraction persists, it may be a call to attend prayerfully to the object of the distraction. For example, a conflict may well continue to surface until it has been resolved.

5. Colloquy: Closing Conversational Prayer

Saint Ignatius was sensitive to the depth of feeling aroused by the contemplation of the suffering Jesus. Although a suggestion for this intimate conversational prayer at the end of each prayer period has been provided, the pray-er is encouraged to let his or her heart speak in an intimate outpouring of feeling, of love and compassion. The pray-er is strongly urged to *be with* Jesus in his resurrection. One may need to pray for the desire to *want* to experience resurrection with Christ. The important thing to remember is that simple presence is primary. Just to be silent in the presence of Christ's resurrection is profound prayer.

Prayer of Love and Praise

Lord my God, when Your love spilled over
into creation
You thought of me.
I am
from love   of love   for love.

Let my heart, O God, always
recognize,
cherish,
and enjoy your goodness in all of creation.

Direct all that is me toward your praise.
Teach me reverence for every person, all things.
Energize me in your service.

Lord God
may nothing ever distract me from your
love . . .
neither health nor sickness
wealth nor poverty
honor nor dishonor
long life nor short life.

May I never seek nor choose to be other
than You intend or wish.   Amen.

my word
is not my own
it is the word
of
the one
who
sent me.

JN 14:24

Week 1, Day 1: Newness

"Christmas is caught forever in the easter event" (71, p. 23).

It is altogether fitting and natural that Jesus would have appeared to his mother after the resurrection, his joyous rebirth. His resurrection completes and brings to fullness the moments when his mother conceived and gave him birth.

Jesus' joyously revealing his resurrected self to his mother holds for us, forever, the beauty and fresh promise of the nativity scene.

The empty womb gave way to and is one with the empty tomb.

Mary's cooperation with God's plan, her courageous surrender to God's Word within her, is the matrix of Jesus' surrender on the cross.

Every authentic new beginning is birthed within the courageous acceptance of a definitive ending.

Jesus really died!

An ending, when embraced, creates the emptiness, the void (Gen. 1:2) essential for the emergence of the new thing to happen (Rev. 21:5). Only in this way can a genuine newness arise, a newness that is not merely a reshuffling of old patterns and values.

Jesus rose to *new* life!

Mary recognizes Jesus in all his gladness and glory.

The greeting of this moment is "Alleluia! Joy to the world!"

Suggested Approach to Prayer: Consolation

+ *Daily prayer pattern:* (See pages 1 and 2.)
  I quiet myself and relax in the presence of God.
  I declare my dependency on God.

+ *Grace:* I ask for a share in the joy of Jesus, risen.

+ *Method:* Contemplation, as on page 3; journaling, as on page 5.
  I place myself before the tomb of Jesus. I allow my feelings and thoughts

to surface as I consider the kind of day it is—whether cold or warm—who is present, the position of the stone.

Leaving the tomb, I make my way to the house where Mary lives. I visualize in detail whether it is large or small, surrounded by a garden or not, the kind of plants in the garden, and so on.

Entering through the door, I catch a glimpse of Mary in her room. I become aware of her clothing, its textures and colors. I note whether the room has any particular fragrance.

As I look at Mary, I recall how I last saw her, faithfully present at Jesus' crucifixion.

I enter Mary's room. I am reverently present, aware of how her profound feelings are manifested in her external expression.

Suddenly, Jesus, risen, comes!

He is radiant with joy and new life!

Mary recognizes him!

I see him; I recognize him!

I see Mary enter into sharing the joy that is Jesus'. I watch Mary's response to Jesus who consoles her. I see how her entire person responds.

Listening and observing carefully, I absorb this scene fully into myself. I open myself totally to allow every detail of this encounter to enter me, to fill each of my senses with this event.

Jesus, resurrected and consoling, turns to me.

I invite Jesus to enter into conversation with me. I beg to share in the joy and consolation of his risen life.

I proceed with this conversation with Jesus, first one speaking and then the other:

Me:

Jesus:

Me:

I write this entire dialogue in my journal.

I let go of any anxiousness concerning this conversation, aware that it is meant only for my eyes.

I enter fully into the exchange between Jesus and me. I present and share my questions and feelings with Jesus.

I allow this dialogue to proceed slowly and to flow naturally. Particularly, I allow space for Jesus to speak. Knowing that I may not hear him immediately, I wait patiently.

+ *Closing:* I pray the Our Father.

+ *Review of prayer:* I highlight or underline those words of the dialogue that have particularly moved me.

+ *Additional suggestion:* I commit myself, in the manner of the consoling Risen Christ, to write a letter or make a phone call to someone in need.

Week 1, Day 2: Love's Song

SONG OF SONGS 2:8–14

I hear my love.
See how he comes
leaping on the mountains,
bounding over the hills.
My love is like a gazelle,
like a young stag.

See where he stands
behind our wall.
He looks in at the window,
he peers through the opening.

My love lifts up his voice,
he says to me,
"Come then, my beloved,
my lovely one, come.
For see, winter is past,
the rains are over and gone.

"Flowers are appearing on the earth.
The season of glad songs has come,
the cooing of the turtledove is heard
in our land.
The fig tree is forming its first figs
and the blossoming vines give out their fragrance.
Come then, my beloved,
my lovely one, come.

"My dove, hiding in the clefts of the rock,
in the coverts of the cliff,
show me your face,
let me hear your voice;
for your voice is sweet
and your face is lovely."

Every lover has a song!

Of all the songs of love that have risen from the human heart, the Song of Songs is undoubtedly the most acclaimed and long enduring.

Richly symbolic, it offers to human experience multiple levels of meaning. In its journey toward love and integrity, the human heart can find in this exquisite song a wealth of consoling images that give hope and reassurance.

It is truly the Song *of* Songs!

It is a song that praises and exalts love as the most creative, the most healing energy in the universe. Throughout this collection of love songs and poetic lyrics, love and union between man and woman is celebrated. The song's images of pursuit, enticement, and promise are images that lovers delight in!

The joy and holiness of love between a woman and a man have always been affirmed within the most authentic traditions of God's people. From the earliest times of the Jewish Scriptures, the marriage union has provided an image of Yahweh's enduring love for God's people, the Israelites. In the Christian Testament, Paul draws on this same image to speak of the intimacy of Christ's love for those who believe in him (Eph. 5:32). In the Spirit of love they are united, in an ongoing creation, into a community of love with the Risen Christ and with each other.

Always the love song is "Come . . . my beloved . . . come." Always "deep is calling to deep" (Ps. 42:7) between hearts and *within* each human heart.

"Come . . . my beloved . . . come" is a song of yearning, yearning for union within ourselves, yearning for the reconciliation of the inner opposing poles that divide and fragment our truest self. We call out to love's voice within ourselves— seeking freedom and healing.

Our entire being seeks union, constantly moving toward an inner wholeness —a weddedness of all the fragments of our lives. And in the wholeness within us is the Divine ultimately met, mysteriously wed; it "grows visible" through our humanness (25, Prologue).

Joyfully we sing the Easter song: "Night truly blessed when heaven is wedded to earth and [we are] reconciled with God" (80, Easter Proclamation, p. 184). Alleluia!

Suggested Approach to Prayer: Energy of Love

+ *Daily prayer pattern:* (See pages 1 and 2.)
  I quiet myself and relax in the presence of God.
  I declare my dependency on God.

+ *Grace:* I ask to enter into the joy and consolation of Jesus, risen.

+ *Method:* Contemplation, as on page 3.
  I form an image of the Risen Christ before me. I see a powerful energy force of consoling love being emitted from his risen body. It is a glowing, spring-like aura, surrounding his entire person.

  I hear Christ beckon me to come near, "Come, my beloved one, come."

  The love power draws me forward. Slowly, I move closer. As I enter into its sphere, I feel the warmth of this love penetrate my body.

  The energy of love moves first upward from my feet. I feel it in my ankles. In my right leg I feel its comforting warmth, and then in my left leg. It enters into the trunk of my body. Every organ is warmed by its touch. I feel my stomach relax, releasing its anxiety. My lungs move in and out freely; my heart, too, beats calmly, rhythmically, quieted by this consoling energy of love moving down my arms, even into my fingertips.

  I continue to hear the words call me closer, "Come, my beloved."

  I feel myself drawn nearer, more deeply within the aura of love.

  I feel the love energy move throughout all the convolutions of my brain. My entire brain has absorbed the energy of love.

  Every cell of my body absorbs this love energy into its center. My entire body is relaxed, embraced in the consolation of love.

  I feel the energy move deep within me, deep within my innermost soul, moving about searching and peering into all the hidden, suppressed areas of woundedness and pain. No memory, no hurt escapes the swift, sure penetration of this consoling force.

  In trust and openness I relax into this embrace, allowing Christ's consoling presence to love and to heal my painful memories, wherever it touches, whether it be a moment in childhood or only yesterday. I allow the painful memory to absorb this healing energy.

This Christ energy knows no bounds. It continues to move throughout my body, my soul, throughout the years of my life.

No walls of time or repression hold back its loving persistence. I sense it moving even into the future, guiding me, protecting me.

Swiftly and gently it moves. No memory, no pain is left untouched.

Embraced and held within this consoling energy, I hear the words of love and promise echo deep within me.

"My lovely one. . . .
winter is past,
the rains are over and gone.

"Flowers are appearing on the earth.
The season of glad songs has come."

I rest in the presence of love.

+ *Closing:* I let my heart respond in praise and thanksgiving. I pray the Our Father.

+ *Review of prayer:* I write in my journal the insights and feelings that have surfaced during this time of prayer.

Week 1, Day 3: Pregnant with Hope

LUKE 1:46–55

And Mary said:

> *My being proclaims your greatness,*
> *and my spirit finds joy in you, God my Savior.*
>
> *For you have looked upon me, your servant, in my*
> *lowliness;*
> *all ages to come shall call me blessed.*
>
> *God, you who are mighty, have done great things for*
> *me.*
> *Holy is your name.*
>
> *Your mercy is from age to age toward those who fear*
> *you.*
>
> *You have shown might with your arm*
> *and confused the proud in their inmost thoughts.*
>
> *You have deposed the mighty from their thrones*
> *and raised the lowly to high places.*
>
> *The hungry you have given every good thing*
> *while the rich you have sent away empty.*
>
> *You have upheld Israel your servant, ever mindful of*
> *your mercy—*
>
> *even as you promised our ancestors;*
> *promised Abraham, Sarah, and their descendants*
> *forever.*

Hope lives in the belly of a pregnant woman!

Pressing toward the twenty-first century, we yearn for a sign of hope. We desperately seek a symbol empowered with the primal energies of our history and traditions. Spiritually and psychically we need a central, core image capable of concentrating the energies of our past with the exigencies of the present and the evolutionary demand of the future.

Contained within the mother's womb is all of the genetic richness of ancestral heritage, as well as the particular endowment of the creative moment of conception, with its "infinite," unique, potential contribution to future generations.

Can it possibly be that the symbol of hope we urgently seek is the pregnant woman? Anthropology says *yes:* "All wandering is from the mother, to the mother, in the mother" (48, p. 36).

Prehistoric cultures were grounded in the cultic awareness of the earth as the Great Mother from whom all life came forth and to whom all life surrendered. Archaeologists continue to uncover artifacts that substantiate the homage that ancient peoples paid to the awesome goddesses of fertility. The recovery of numerous small feminine figurines used in cultic fertility worship has established without a doubt that the symbol of the Great Mother was core to the shaping of neolithic cultures.

Our own biblical heritage has preserved for us the profound symbolism of the pregnant woman. Using strong imagery, the author of Revelation speaks of the woman "robed with the sun, standing on the moon, and on her head a crown of twelve stars. She was pregnant, and in labour, crying aloud in the pangs of childbirth" (Rev. 12:1–2).

Our contemporary culture can benefit from a reappropriation of this image of birthing that contains so many levels of meaningful interpretation. The woman, as mother, is Israel who brought forth the Messiah. She is also the image of the Church. Although it is probable that the author of Revelation did not have Mary, the Mother of Jesus, in mind when he created this magnificent image, the liturgy of the Church has consistently applied it to Mary.

Mary, the Mother of Jesus, is always the woman pregnant with the Word (Luke 8:19–21).

God, active and present throughout all ages, mindful of our every need, has chosen Mary to collaborate in the gestation of justice in the world.

As "spokeswoman of the anawim" (16, p. 357)—the poor—Mary models in her surrender the receptivity essential for the transformation of all our spiritual and material poverty, blindness, and hunger into the fullness and joy of the risen presence of Jesus. Through him, "nothing is impossible" (Gen. 18:14; Luke 1:37).

The Advent mother awaiting birth is one with the Easter mother awaiting and welcoming the new life of Christ's risen presence. Together they call each of us to enter into the joyous song of exultation and praise that was Mary's. Her song is the call to rejoice in gratitude for the ever-present, merciful God of love who offered to her, and offers to us, a timeless, pregnant covenantal intimacy, an intimacy rooted in mutual promise and surrender.

Suggested Approach to Prayer: Praying with Mary

+ *Daily prayer pattern:* (See pages 1 and 2.)
I quiet myself and relax in the presence of God.
I declare my dependency on God.

+ *Grace:* I ask, in the spirit of Mary, to enter into the joy of Jesus, risen.

+ *Method:* Meditation, as on page 3.
I read and reread slowly Luke 1:46–55, allowing myself to share in Mary's gladness at Jesus' joy of being resurrected.

I visualize her present as Jesus, risen, stands before her in his happiness.

I listen attentively to her every word of praise of God for his goodness to her, for his promise to her and to all generations.

Sensitive to the nuance of feelings being expressed, I absorb the words as if they are my own.

I allow the words to descend deep within me until they locate and touch a center of resonance.

+ *Closing:* I speak simply and lovingly to Jesus, offering my own magnificat of praise and thanksgiving. I pray the Our Father.

+ *Review of prayer:* I record in my journal the insights and feelings that have surfaced during this time of prayer.

Week 1, Day 4: The Birth of Joy

LUKE 1:46–55, see Week 1, Day 3.

Mary's life of surrender made it possible for God to draw her wholly into the unlimited joy of the Spirit. Her receptivity released into the world a song of promise.

Alive within each human heart is a magnificat awaiting its full expression. In each of us the great mother-spirit beckons us forward into a joy that is the complete expression of all God uniquely intends for us.

This movement into blessedness, and the tasks that define it, have been for all people the very stuff of their life. It is in the ordinary that this journey evolves. It is in the ordinary that one writes one's own particular life script.

A certain oneness of experience unites all our stories. To listen to a story is to expand and deepen our own experience as we live into, live with, and learn from the shared experience of another. Through the gift of imagination we truly have an experience that has the capacity to guide and affirm our own story.

A particularly delightful form of storytelling is the myth, as it has come to us from ancient times. The Greek myth of Psyche's journey of life is unusually adaptable in portraying the challenge that each person must encounter as she or he enters into the transforming dynamics of holiness (52).

One dimension of this insightful story involves the four tasks given to Psyche, whose name means "soul." Aphrodite, the goddess of love, begrudgingly promises Psyche that upon the completion of the four tasks, she will be reunited with her lover. Psyche will then enter into the fullness of joy.

Psyche's first task is to sort through a huge pile of many kinds of seeds. This is to be completed before evening. Psyche is overwhelmed by the magnitude of such a task. There is no possible way she can sort through all the seeds. She sits down. Suddenly an entire colony of ants comes to her aid. With a flurry of industrious precision, they sort the seeds for her.

The second task before Psyche is dangerous. She is to bring back from the vicious Sun Rams a bit of their golden fleece. She collapses at the mere idea. She even entertains thoughts of throwing herself into the river. At the crucial moment, the reeds in the river speak to her, advising her on how to collect the fleece safely. They tell her to pluck the fleece from the bramble bushes that the rams pass through. She is relieved to know that she can obtain the fleece without directly encountering the dangerous rams.

For the third task, Aphrodite tells Psyche to fill a crystal goblet from the river Styx, which leads into hell. Psyche is horrified, for the river is guarded by frightful monsters. She can foresee no way of getting close enough to the river to fill the goblet. Suddenly, from out of the sky, a magnificent eagle comes to her assistance. He flies over the river, surveying the whole situation. He focuses intently on a single spot, and with swift sureness, he swoops down and easily fills her goblet.

Psyche has successfully completed three of the four tasks! Aphrodite is furious!

However, Psyche's most challenging task remains. She must make the dark journey into the terrifying underworld to obtain a cask of beauty ointment for Aphrodite. Once more Psyche collapses. This time her helper is truly remarkable and entirely unexpected. Her helper is not a living being or anything of nature; it is a tower! The tower lays out a plan for her. She is given two coins and two pieces of barley bread, with specific directions not to use these for others who will make demands on her as she travels downward. The coins will serve as her passage to and from the underworld; the bread is to be used to pacify the dogs that guard the entrance to and exit from the underworld.

After surviving many perilous adventures, Psyche returns to the surface of the world. Her success is thwarted, however, by her own self-interest. She deliberately opens the cask that she knows is not meant for her but for the goddess of love. Not beauty but a deep sleep descends upon her. Psyche appears dead.

Finally, Eros, Psyche's lover, comes to Psyche's rescue. Lovingly he wipes the sleep from Psyche and carries her off to heaven. The two of them are married and live happily ever after! In time they give birth to a beautiful daughter whom they name Pleasure, and some call Joy. Such is the story that the ancients told.

In the fullness of time, Mary gave birth to joy; we are all called to birth joy. There is no birthing of joy without being faithful to the labor of transformation and without the tasks of ordering, focusing, discernment, and reconciliation.

In each human heart, joy is awaiting its birth.

With Mary, we too can sing, "My being proclaims your greatness, / and my spirit finds joy in you, God my Savior."

Suggested Approach to Prayer: Life's Tasks

+ *Daily prayer pattern:* (See pages 1 and 2.)
I quiet myself and relax in the presence of God.
I declare my dependency on God.

+ *Grace:* I ask to be strengthened in the presence of the Risen Christ and in the spirit of Mary.

+ *Method:* Meditation, as on page 3.
I quietly reread Luke 1:46–55, Mary's Magnificat.

In the spirit of Mary's surrender, I prayerfully reflect on Psyche's journey in order to glean the Spirit's wisdom and direction for my own life.

I consider how I am called to discern answers to questions such as the following at this point in my journey:

- Where in my life am I experiencing the seed of greatest confusion of values?
- Where in my life do I experience being overwhelmed and out of touch with my feelings?
- Where in my life do I most doubt my own motives or experience them as conflicting with each other?
- How can I enlist the aid of the Spirit in sorting through and bringing order to these many "seeds"?

To bring order and thus complete this first task, I will . . .

I consider how I am called to gather the courage, power, and strength within me:

- Where do I tend to give away my power, either to others or in particular situations?
- In what areas of my life is my desire for status, fame, fortune, and control addicting and destructive?

- With whom do I engage in a power struggle?
- What kind of power do I most identify with and seek to emulate?
- Where is it that I am *ram-like?*
- Where within myself do I most experience a power that is compassionate?
- In what ways do I claim my power; how do I most manifest my own valor and courage?

For this second task, in order to lay claim to the power within me in a way that is not destructive to myself or others, I will . . .

I consider how I am called to focus and choose among the myriad possibilities that life's journey places before me:

- In what areas of my life do I fragment my peace, energy, and intent by indulging in dissatisfaction and discontentment?
- At what times do I tend to take on too much at once, thereby deflecting and dissipating my focus?
- Where am I most shattered because of my inflated or oversensitive ego?
- What small events and experiences give me joy and bring meaning to my life?

In order to complete this third task of giving focus to my life, I will . . .

I consider how I am called to attend to my own life's journey toward freedom in God's Spirit:

- How and when am I distracted from focusing on God's unique intent for me through my preoccupation with subtly, or not so subtly, interfering in, controlling, meddling in, "fixing" the lives of others?
- When do I act contrary to my own well-being by indiscriminately saying yes to others' demands on my time, space, and gifts?
- When am I unfaithful in attending to my own inner hunger through misplaced generosity and kindness, giving to others out of my need to be needed or to control?
- When do I drug myself into a lifeless sleep through an addictive preoccupation with impressing others: for example, through external appearances, possessions, clothes, cosmetics, position, achievements, degrees, success, status, popularity?

- When am I untrue to my inner spirit by taking on the feelings, opinions, ways, and practices of others or by living out of and up to the expectations of other people?
- How am I experiencing myself being drawn to and moving toward more balance and centeredness?

To accomplish this fourth task of fidelity to self, I will . . .

Like Psyche, I too await the gift of God; like Mary, I await and open myself to the joy of God's Spirit—a spirit of discernment, a spirit of power, a spirit of wisdom, and a spirit of faithfulness.

+ *Closing:* I pray the Magnificat as my own prayer.

+ *Review of prayer:* I note in my journal the directions that have been revealed to me as part of my task throughout the time of prayer.

Week 1, Day 5: Repetition

Suggested Approach to Prayer

+ *Daily prayer pattern:* (See pages 1 and 2.)
I quiet myself and relax in the presence of God.
I declare my dependency on God.

+ *Grace:* I ask for a deep sharing in the joy of the Risen Christ.

+ *Method:* Repetition, as on page 6.

In preparation, I review my prayer periods by reading my journal entries for the past week. I select for repetition the period of prayer in which I was most deeply moved or the one in which I experienced a lack of emotional response or the one in which I was grasped with insight or the one in which I experienced confusion. I use the method with which I initially approached the passage. I open myself to hear again God's word to me in that particular passage.

+ *Review of prayer:* I write in my journal any feelings, experiences, or insights that have surfaced in this second listening.

Week 1, Day 6: The New Galilee

MARK 16:1–8

When the Sabbath was over, Mary of Magdala, Mary the mother of James, and Salome, bought spices with which to go and anoint him. And very early in the morning on the first day of the week they went to the tomb when the sun had risen.

They had been saying to one another, "Who will roll away the stone for us from the entrance to the tomb?" But when they looked they saw that the stone—which was very big—had already been rolled back. On entering the tomb they saw a young man in a white robe seated on the right-hand side, and they were struck with amazement. But he said to them, "There is no need to be so amazed. You are looking for Jesus of Nazareth, who was crucified; he has risen, he is not here. See, here is the place where they laid him. But you must go and tell his disciples and Peter, 'He is going ahead of you to Galilee; that is where you will see him, just as he told you.'" And the women came out and ran away from the tomb because they were frightened out of their wits; and they said nothing to anyone, for they were afraid.

What *life* do we seek that compels us to look in the places of death?

Why do tombs exert such a magnetic attraction for us? In Moscow, people take pilgrimages to the Tomb of Lenin. In England, people reverently visit the graves of kings and poets interred at Westminster Abbey. A visit to Egypt would not be complete without seeing the Pyramids, tombs of ancient kings and queens. At the Arlington National Cemetery a steady flow of people visit the Tomb of the Unknown Soldier, as well as the graves of John F. Kennedy and his brother Robert.

Who are *we* looking for (John 20:15)?

When Mary of Magdala, Mary the mother of James, and Salome went to the tomb, they were conscious only of honoring the memory of Jesus. They were met by the unexpected! Concerned about how to roll away the stone sealing the entrance to the tomb, they found, to their amazement, that it had already been rolled away. They expected to anoint the corpse of Jesus, but found the tomb was empty. Their spices were no longer necessary.

Nothing was as the women had planned and prepared for. The silence they had anticipated was broken by the appearance and clear direction of an angel. The time of mourning they had so carefully set aside ended abruptly when they were commanded, "You must go." The place of death had become the site of emergence. Jesus was no longer sealed and found in death. He was gone and his absence impressed the stupendous reality upon the women that the crucified one was alive. Christ had risen. The women, and we, will not find the living one among the dead (Luke 24:5). We, too, must attend to the angel's message; we, too, must proceed to "Galilee." There we will find what we seek.

The summons to Galilee, the original site of Jesus' first call to his disciples, now becomes both a command and a promise. In Galilee his presence will be most visible to us. Galilee, which also represents the place of reconciliation between Jew and Gentile, now symbolically extends to the world a promise of peace and oneness made possible in Christ's presence. "Galilee" is the fullness of community that is to characterize the end times, Jesus' final coming.

We are an "in-between people" that exist in the "now" of the resurrection, and at the same time, in the "not-yet" of the final coming. We are always "on the way" to Galilee, for we are an Easter people living in the shadow of the cross.

Jesus is risen, sometimes hidden, and, at times, wonderfully present, though not fully revealed. The need to trust and to surrender in faith is our great task!

The resurrection offers no panacea. It does not deliver the believer from the harsh realities of life's struggles. Rather, in the midst of pain, disappointment, and frustration, it offers the reassurance and affirmation of the triumph of goodness over evil.

To realize the implications of the resurrection is to experience with the women the reversal of all our expectations. The resurrection is a fear-filled experience that exposes our vulnerabilities and tests our trust. The awareness and awe of the possibility before us draws us into prayerful pondering (Luke 2:19). Simultaneously, the power and energy released by Christ's resurrection urges us to go beyond our fears and to enter into the creating of community, the Galilee of the New Age.

Suggested Approach to Prayer: Entering the Tomb

+ *Daily prayer pattern:* (See pages 1 and 2.)
I quiet myself and relax in the presence of God.
I declare my dependency on God.

+ *Grace:* I ask to share deeply in the joy of the Risen Christ.

+ *Method:* Contemplation, as on page 3.
With Mary of Magdala, Mary the mother of James, and Salome, I go to the tomb of Jesus.

I take note of the kind of morning it is, if it is totally light or if the shadows of night still linger. My senses heighten as I call myself to the awareness of the moment; that is, of the warmth or coolness of the morning air, the fragrance of the spices, and the mood of the small group.

Listening to the questioning of the women, I ponder my own question. Watching their amazement at the stone's being rolled away, I am aware of my own response.

I enter with the women into the tomb. I follow the conversation with the angel, noting in detail my own feeling response as well as any insights that surface.

I leave the tomb with the women. What are the questions, the feelings, and the hopes that fill my heart?

+ *Closing:* I enter into conversation with the Risen Christ, opening the questions and the hopes of my life to him. I pray the Our Father.

+ *Review of prayer:* In my journal I note the feelings and insights that have surfaced during my prayer.

Week 2, Day 1: The Earth Quakes

MATT. 28:1–8

After the Sabbath, and towards dawn on the first day of the week, Mary of Magdala and the other Mary went to visit the sepulchre. And suddenly there was a violent earthquake, for an angel of the Lord, descending from heaven, came and rolled away the stone and sat on it. His face was like lightning, his robe white as snow. The guards were so shaken by fear of him that they were like dead men. But the angel spoke; and he said to the women, "There is no need for you to be afraid. I know you are looking for Jesus, who was crucified. He is not here, for he has risen, as he said he would. Come and see the place where he lay, then go quickly and tell his disciples, 'He has risen from the dead and now he is going ahead of you to Galilee; that is where you will see him.' Look! I have told you." Filled with awe and great joy the women came quickly away from the tomb and ran to tell the disciples.

An earthquake announcing good news? Impossible! Impossible? Innumerable major quakes have shocked our earth during recent years. China, Mexico, and Colombia have been the sites of untold death and destruction. Meanwhile, the world remains on constant alert for the predicted disaster at the San Andreas Fault. It takes a long view to perceive an earthquake as announcing any good news! Seismologists, however, tell us that earthquakes are essential for the renewal of the earth, that through the energy released from the earth's fiery center, the crust of the earth is broken, forming new land. Earthquakes are part of God's unfolding creation.

A long view is required to trust that in the upheaval of a quake a new beginning is taking place, that the Spirit is actually hovering over the chaos (Gen. 1:2). It is not surprising, then, that in the narration of the resurrection, the angel's message from God is heralded by an earthquake. Something radically new is being announced. As the strata of the earth shifts with the pressure of creation, the stone before the tomb is displaced, disclosing an entire shift of consciousness for those who believe.

Standing before the emptiness of the tomb, the sudden bright illumination of the meaning of Jesus' absence is nearly overwhelming. In fact, the guards are frozen in the paralysis of incomprehension. But for those who have come to the tomb seeking Jesus, the word is clear and reassuring.

"'There is no need for you to be afraid. . . . he has risen from the dead.'"

The Jesus they knew and loved is fulfilling his promise. He has broken the bonds of death. The shattering, convulsive experience of his crucifixion (Matt. 27:51) has now become, in the light of the opened and empty tomb, the enduring reality of his presence.

Suggested Approach to Prayer: Before the Tomb

+ *Daily prayer pattern:* (See pages 1 and 2.)
I quiet myself and relax in the presence of God.
I declare my dependency on God.

+ *Grace:* I ask to experience joy and the healing presence of Jesus, risen.

+ *Method:* Contemplation, as on page 3.
Within a great imaginary circle, I gather all the people I know and love. I am aware of all the brokenness, as well as the joy, that each one carries in his or her being.

Into the circle, I gather all the diverse peoples of our earth, with their pain, frustration, joys and hopes.

I see myself present within this vast array of God's creation.

In the center of the circle, I see the empty tomb of Jesus.

Standing before the tomb, I am warmed by the bright illumination of God's Word, radiating outward. I allow myself to absorb the powerful energy emanating from the tomb. I hear the words, "Do not be afraid," resonate deep within me.

Slowly I become aware of the energy of God's revealing power reaching out to embrace all those who are gathered within the circle. I watch them as, one by one, they become aware of the implications of the empty tomb.

Gradually, I see and experience the healing of a promise realized. The posture of brokenness begins to give way to a posture of hope. Tense features soften.

One by one, I see each person filled with the joy of knowing that Jesus has risen from the dead. I share fully in the joy of this great gift.

As with one voice, as in a chorus, together we sing, "He is not here . . . he has risen . . . Alleluia!"

+ *Closing:* I speak intimately and simply to the Risen Christ, present with me. I pray the Our Father.

+ *Review of prayer:* In my journal I note the insights and feelings that have surfaced during my prayer.

Week 2, Day 2: Eyes of Love

JOHN 20:1–10

It was very early on the first day of the week and still dark, when Mary of Magdala came to the tomb. She saw that the stone had been moved away from the tomb and came running to Simon Peter and the other disciple, the one whom Jesus loved. "They have taken the Lord out of the tomb," she said, "and we don't know where they have put him."

So Peter set out with the other disciple to go to the tomb. They ran together, but the other disciple, running faster than Peter, reached the tomb first; he bent down and saw the linen cloths lying on the ground, but did not go in. Simon Peter, following him, also came up, went into the tomb, saw the linen cloths lying on the ground and also the cloth that had been over his head; this was not with the linen cloths but rolled up in a place by itself. Then the other disciple who had reached the tomb first also went in; he saw and he believed. Till this moment they had still not understood the scripture, that he must rise from the dead. The disciples then went back home.

To love is to see. Love is the prism through which sensitivity is refracted. The eyes of one who loves see life's deepest reality.

Two people can observe the same thing and have two different interpretations. Each person comes with a vision colored by whatever darkness or light she or he carries within herself or himself. Only through the eyes of love is truth made luminous and clear.

To see with love is to believe. At the heart of belief is love: the word *belief* actually has as its root the Teutonic word *lief,* meaning "love." To believe is to live *by* love.

Love drew Mary of Magdala in the early morning to the tomb of Jesus, the predawn darkness poignantly mirrored in the darkness of her own spirit. Her experience of the absence of Jesus had created within her a keen sense of loss and bewilderment. In the darkness, Mary saw only an empty tomb. She ran, in desolation and panic, to tell Peter and the other disciple what she feared had happened: "'They have taken the Lord.'"

The fear-flight reaction of Mary incited the disciples to a swift response of love. They went eagerly to the tomb to see with their own eyes. The energy of their love impelled them to great haste; it readied their vision for the unexpected. Both entered the tomb. Both saw the funeral cloths of Jesus.

It was appropriate that these two key disciples were together at that moment of insight. They were there not as rivals but as friends and fellow disciples. As leaders they had significant roles in the ancient Church. "The particular manifestation of the Spirit granted to each one is to be used for the general good" (1 Cor. 12:7). Peter was one who came to be known as the shepherd of the flock (John 21:15ff.). The other disciple was one who demonstrated the primacy of love and provided us with the ideal model of discipleship. Because of his great love for Christ, he was known as the Beloved Disciple. In the darkness of the tomb it was his eyes that saw clearly the deeper reality of the emptiness. With the sensitivity of love, he grasped the truth. In that moment of illumination, the teaching of the Scriptures that Christ "would rise from the dead" came to light, and he believed.

Gifted by God with the eyes of love, the Beloved Disciple experienced that the Jesus whom he knew, loved, and had been taught by had not been removed from him by death. He saw that Jesus, now glorified, was more deeply present to him than ever.

Through the eyes of love, the Beloved Disciple was gifted with an acute awareness that the Christ of earth is one with the Divine presence.

The Word became flesh,
he lived among us,
and we saw his glory.
        (John 1:14)

In the tomb, at the moment of belief, the Beloved Disciple saw earth and heaven as one; who sees me sees God (John 14:9).

Suggested Approach to Prayer: The Inner Eye

+ *Daily prayer pattern:* (See pages 1 and 2.)
I quiet myself and relax in the presence of God.
I declare my dependency on God.

+ *Grace:* I ask to share in the joy and healing presence of Jesus, risen, and to rejoice in his joy.

+ *Method:* Meditation, as on page 3.
The cliché, "What you see is what you get," is misleading. It would be more accurate to say, "What you see is not *all* that you get."

Things are not always what they seem to be at first sight. Only with the inner eye, the eye of the Spirit of love, can we see the whole picture. Most frequently our field of vision is narrow. With a partial, selective view we see only what is positive and acceptable and deny the rest, or we may focus on and overemphasize the negative. Either way we miss the deeper reality, the greater potential. A life lived with a vision of wholeness is a life poised in the clarity and balance of love.

With anticipation, and confident of the Risen Christ, I form an image of myself entering into the emptiness of the tomb of Jesus.

I call to mind, in detail, a situation or event in my life that appeared positive but was, in reality, negative and destructive.

I also recall in detail a situation or event that appeared negative but was, in reality, life-giving.

I reflect on what helped me to see with clarity the deeper reality of each situation or event.

Taking another step, I enter more deeply into the tomb, into my own inner darkness.

I deliberately call to mind the grace I am seeking, that is, to see, through love, the presence of the Risen Christ in the totality of my experience.

In my journal I list the positive qualities that I most admire in others. In the second column, I list those negative characteristics in others that I find most offensive.

Positive	Negative
/	/
/	/
/	/
/	/

I consider and write what each one of the positive qualities would look like negatively if carried to the extreme: for example, kind/ingratiating.

I consider and write the positive energy strengths not readily recognizable within the negative characteristics: for example, meanness/tough love.

In the presence of the Spirit, I continue my prayer. I consider each of the qualities and characteristics that I have listed, putting a check by those with which I identify. With courage and unrelenting honesty, I claim ownership for those I recognize within myself.

I visualize myself in the presence of the Risen Christ. I surrender *all* of who I am to Christ. I ask for his direction so that I can discern how his love calls me to clarity and the balance of love.

In the Spirit of love, I determine the following action and write it in my journal:

In order to temper the positive qualities within me, I will . . .

In order to tap the potential strength of the negative characteristics within me, I will . . .

+ *Closing:* I make acts of surrender to the Risen Christ, present with me. I pray the Our Father.

+ *Review of prayer:* In my journal I write about the course of action that I have decided upon, with the intention of rereading these words regularly.

Week 2, Day 3: Hear and Believe

JOHN 20:11–18

But Mary was standing outside near the tomb, weeping. Then, as she wept, she stooped to look inside, and saw two angels in white sitting where the body of Jesus had been, one at the head, the other at the feet. They said, "Woman, why are you weeping?" "They have taken my Lord away," she replied, "and I don't know where they have put him." As she said this she turned round and saw Jesus standing there, though she did not realise that it was Jesus. Jesus said to her, "Woman, why are you weeping? Who are you looking for?" Supposing him to be the gardener, she said, "Sir, if you have taken him away, tell me where you have put him, and I will go and remove him." Jesus said, "Mary!" She turned round then and said to him in Hebrew, "Rabbuni!"—which means Master. Jesus said to her, "Do not cling to me, because I have not yet ascended to the Father. But go and find my brothers, and tell them: I am ascending to my Father and your Father, to my God and your God." So Mary of Magdala told the disciples, "I have seen the Lord," and that he had said these things to her.

Is belief so far removed from unbelief; is love so far from hate? Is not hope only a moment away from despair, and does not joy live side by side with tears?

There is the space between, where all things touch and meet; a word, one simple word, has the infinite potential to unleash power for life to renew itself.

"Mary."

To the woman in tears, bound in unbelief, the one word spoken was her name, "Mary." The moment she heard, she believed. In the sound of his voice saying her name she recognized Jesus. Undoubtedly, this meeting in the garden of the resurrection is one of the greatest recognition scenes in all of history.

"Rabbuni." Mary's spontaneous response of love filled the morning air. The

Jesus whose death she grieved now stood before her. The compassionate Jesus who, through the healing of forgiveness, had released her into new meaning and purpose of life was not dead! The compelling Jesus who claimed her loyalty for his mission still lived!

He called her by name, "Mary."

In response, she called him, "Rabbuni."

This encounter with the Risen Christ reopened to Mary the possibility of the wonderful joy of friendship with him (John 15:15).

In the garden of the resurrection, a new time—new creation—came into being.

Jesus' death, which initially must have been a devastating experience for Mary, had now become in an unsurpassed way life-giving. As Jesus stood glorified before Mary, her sorrows and incomprehension were shed like a skin that no longer fits. In its place, she was clothed with the power and the energy of an intimate inner knowledge of and love for Christ (Luke 24:49).

In the Garden of Eden, humankind tried to grasp for themselves all knowledge of good and evil. The serpent, the most subtle of all the wild beasts, promised: "You will not die! . . . your eyes will be opened and you will be like gods, knowing good from evil" (Gen. 3:4-5). Instead, humankind was cast into darkness. But out of Eden, out of the seduction of the serpent, and out of the darkness—this "happy fault" (80, Easter Proclamation, p. 179)—came the true and glorious light of Jesus' risen presence, visible and accessible.

Moses lifted up the serpent in the desert, so that all who saw were healed. Paradoxically the serpent became the symbol of healing. Now Jesus has been lifted up. All who see and hear his word and believe are fully restored as children of God (John 3:13-14).

The chaos and sin of the Garden of Eden is not so far removed from the grace and joy of the resurrection.

Adam and Eve grasped for total knowledge. Mary is tempted to cling to Jesus, to find in him the security and comfort of the time before the resurrection. Jesus calls and empowers Mary to a tenderness that does not grasp and cling. Tenderness conceives and gives life. Grasping and clinging strangle and abort life's energy.

But, in the garden of the resurrection, in the Spirit of the Risen Jesus, all things are new. Jesus draws Mary to respond to his presence with the eyes and ears of love, which will empower her not to cling to him but to reach out to others with the good news of God's unfolding creation.

The recognition scene between Jesus and Mary is dramatically lived out in the circle of every life. Jesus speaks each one's name. He stands before us in glory and draws us to new life, empowerment to reach out to others.

As we hear our name pronounced and as we respond in trust, recognition and reconciliation come together. In each moment of convergence, all of creation—past, present, and to come—share in and are fortified by the transforming energy released by this consoling communion. Rippling through history, a silent alleluia resounds, carrying the message, "Go . . . tell" the others.

Suggested Approach to Prayer: Christ Speaks My Name

+ *Daily prayer pattern:* (See pages 1 and 2.)
I quiet myself and relax in the presence of God.
I declare my dependency on God.

+ *Grace:* I ask to share in the joy of Jesus, risen.

+ *Method:* Contemplation, as on page 3.
I am with Mary of Magdala as she stands weeping outside the tomb. Aware of the early morning hour, I notice the surroundings in detail—the rising sun, whether the morning air is warm or cool, the sounds of the morning, the scents in the air, the colors of nature as the day unfolds.

Noting that the stone is rolled back, I approach the tomb and touch the walls, feeling whether they are rough or smooth.

With Mary, I stoop and look into the tomb. I see the two angels and form an image of them in great detail. I hear them speak to Mary and ask her why she is crying. I listen to her desperate and sad response as she tells them that someone has taken her Lord away.

I become aware of another presence in our midst. I hear him address Mary with the same question, "Why are you weeping?" I hear her demand, "If you have taken him away, tell me where you have put him."

Then, I hear him respond with one word, "Mary."

I see Mary's face light up with amazement and joy as the sound of her name awakens within her the recognition of the Jesus whom she loves.

Jesus turns to me. He asks me where in my heart I am weeping, where I am experiencing his absence. I spend time reflecting on his questions, allowing them to resonate deep within me.

I hear Jesus speak my name, "_____." I surrender in trust to his word. I allow the timbre of his voice to sensitively reverberate throughout my entire self.

As the sound of his voice filters through my being, all the areas of void are filled with his presence.

+ *Closing:* I rest in the joy of the renewing presence of the Risen Christ, in the joy of his joy.

+ *Review of prayer:* I note in my journal the feelings and insights that have surfaced during this time of prayer.

Week 2, Day 4: Future Promise, Present Reality

ISA. 30:18–26

But Yahweh is waiting to be gracious to you,
the Exalted One, to take pity on you,
for Yahweh is a God of fair judgement;
blessed are all who hope in him.

Yes, people of Zion living in Jerusalem,
you will weep no more.
He will be gracious to you when your cry for help rings out;
as soon as he hears it, he will answer you.
When the Lord has given you the bread of suffering
       and the water of distress,
he who is your teacher will hide no longer,
and you will see your teacher with your own eyes.
Your ears will hear these words behind you,
"This is the way, keep to it,"
whether you turn to right or left.
You will hold unclean the silverplating of your idols
and the goldplating of your images.
You will throw them away like the polluted things they are,
shouting after them, "Good riddance!"
He will send rain for the seed you sow in the ground,
and the bread that the ground provides will be rich and
       nourishing.
That day your cattle will graze in wide pastures.
Oxen and donkeys that work the land
will eat for fodder wild sorrel,
spread by the shovel-load and fork-load.
On every lofty mountain, on every high hill
there will be streams and water-courses, on the day of the
       great slaughter
when the strongholds fall.

Then moonlight will be bright as sunlight
and sunlight itself be seven times brighter
—like the light of seven days in one—
on the day Yahweh dresses his people's wound
and heals the scars of the blows they have received.

Can you imagine awakening to a day on which the sun shines with the brilliance of seven days in one? The energy released on such a day would be incredible!

Consider the magnitude of the amount of solar power received on a daily basis needed simply to sustain the various life forms of the planet earth. The concentration of seven days of energy with its resulting synergistic effect would be of immense proportions. One might dare to speculate that a convergence of this nature would set free a power that might approximate the big bang from which, astrophysicists claim, our universe was given birth fifteen billion years ago.

In the Jewish Scriptures, seven times anything implies immensity and incredible scope. When we see our teacher face to face, Isaiah promises, all things will be regenerated. In the sevenfold radiance of the light, every cycle of nature will be enriched and will yield itself to the plan of the Creator. The fecundity of the earth will amaze beyond any expectation.

Through the release of this creative energy, a reordering of all life in God would begin. Every realm of life would be energized and move toward oneness and healing. A clarification of direction and purpose would be apparent and magnetic. Every deflection and addicting counterforce that pulls at the hungry human heart would be immediately rejected as pseudosatisfying. Everyone existing in the exile of homelessness and despair would discover within this energy the deepest core of his or her identity. The ultimate loneliness of fragmentation and alienation, the dark inheritance of every person, would serve as the catalyst for the entry of God's unitive and purifying light. No wound would be unattended, no pain unconsoled. God's energy would pierce, as a surgeon's laser, restoring, renewing—re-creating!

Truly it would be a day of Yahweh!

It would be an empowerment that would bring "to fulfillment the tremendous potentiality locked in every atom of matter" (71, p. 119).

God's promise would be fulfilled.

What was the future promise for the people of Isaiah's time is present reality for those of us who live in Christian Testament times.

The good news is that this love energy that promises fulfillment is present now. From the beginning of creation this energy has mysteriously always been present and gaining momentum as it awaited its moment of release into the world.

Jesus Christ is *the Moment*, first fruit of the new creative action of God. His life, death, and resurrection is the inner dynamic force of the reordering that moves all creation toward completion. To believe in and to embrace the presence of the Risen Christ is to be empowered by the infusion of the sevenfold gifts of God's own Spirit—Light unlimited!

We are a people in process, vulnerable and waiting; as an in-between people of the not-yet-fullness, we live our life in expectant hope.

Suggested Approach to Prayer: The Insatiable Darkness

+ *Daily prayer pattern:* (See pages 1 and 2.)
  I quiet myself and relax in the presence of God.
  I declare my dependency on God.

+ *Grace:* I ask to share in the joy of Jesus, risen.

+ *Method:* Contemplation, as on page 3.
  I imagine within myself the inner core of my loneliness and alienation like a black, empty hole.

  I experience this black hole of emptiness exerting an extraordinary gravitational pull on my inner energies. I envision all the energy within me being drawn into and swallowed up by the darkness.

  I see my energies swirling about in disturbed confusion, gradually creating the mirage of halo-like light. I see the energies whirling downward, disappearing out of sight into the void. The black hole continues to draw energy, is never satisfied, yet emits no true light.

Finally, exhausted, I allow myself to experience the total depletion of my own energy, sinking into and surrendering to my own nothingness. I see the black hole quietly awaiting more energy; in absolute hunger it waits. There is no more energy!

From within the emptiness and the hunger, I pray in a mantralike manner, "Come, Lord Jesus." Repeating this prayer over and over, I focus on each word.

Gradually I become aware of a power other than my own. I allow this power to enter into the blackness as I continue to repeat the prayer, "Come, Lord Jesus." The power grows within.

The core of blackness begins to warm. I pray. Slowly I see a pencil point of light deep within its center. I pray, "Come, Lord Jesus." The light grows stronger yet. I see it now, having risen to the rim of what was previously the dark hole.

I continue to pray, "Come, Lord Jesus." I see the core now as a core of light; I see it as a small sphere of light. It pulsates with every beat of my own heart. Energy and warmth begin to be given out from the center.

As I pray, energy is emitted, and as if directed by some unseen gyro-pilot it moves with swift precision to every localized area of stress and woundedness held bound within my body.

I pray, "Come, Lord Jesus." The healing, life-giving infusion of this new energy continues moving rapidly and accurately throughout my body. Gradually I experience my whole being refreshed and restored. I rest within the warmth of this energy.

+ *Closing:* In gratitude I reflect and embrace the loneliness, the emptiness, and the hunger knowing in a new way that "only God can raise the dead, and God can only raise the dead" (75, p. 119). I pray the Our Father.

+ *Review of prayer:* In my journal, I write whatever insights and feelings have surfaced within this time of prayer.

Week 2, Day 5: The Blind Spot

LUKE 24:13–35

Now that very same day, two of them were on their way to a village called Emmaus, seven miles from Jerusalem, and they were talking together about all that had happened. And it happened that as they were talking together and discussing it, Jesus himself came up and walked by their side; but their eyes were prevented from recognising him. He said to them, "What are all these things that you are discussing as you walk along?" They stopped, their faces downcast.

Then one of them, called Cleopas, answered him, "You must be the only person staying in Jerusalem who does not know the things that have been happening there these last few days." He asked, "What things?" They answered, "All about Jesus of Nazareth, who showed himself a prophet powerful in action and speech before God and the whole people; and how our chief priests and our leaders handed him over to be sentenced to death, and had him crucified. Our own hope had been that he would be the one to set Israel free. And this is not all: two whole days have now gone by since it all happened; and some women from our group have astounded us: they went to the tomb in the early morning, and when they could not find the body, they came back to tell us they had seen a vision of angels who declared he was alive. Some of our friends went to the tomb and found everything exactly as the women had reported, but of him they saw nothing."

Then he said to them, "You foolish men! So slow to believe all that the prophets have said! Was it not necessary that the Christ should suffer before entering into his glory?" Then, starting with Moses and going through all the prophets, he explained to them the passages throughout the scriptures that were about himself.

When they drew near to the village to which they were going, he made as if to go on; but they pressed him to stay with them saying, "It is nearly evening, and the day is almost over." So he went in to stay with them. Now while he was with them at table, he took the bread and said the blessing; then he broke it and handed it to them. And their eyes were opened and they recognised him; but he had vanished from their sight. Then they said to each other, "Did not our hearts burn within us as he talked to us on the road and explained the scriptures to us?"

They set out that instant and returned to Jerusalem. There they found the Eleven assembled together with their companions, who said to them, "The Lord has indeed risen and has appeared to Simon." Then they told their story of what had happened on the road and how they had recognised him at the breaking of bread.

Bad news is not *always* bad news. How we look at it and what we see depends on our knowledge and insight.

Ignorance and slowness of understanding have the power to impel one down a road of confusion and disillusionment. The two travelers on the road to Emmaus are disappointed and sad. Their hearts are heavy with the bad news that the one they loved and looked to as their holy and charismatic leader has suffered a premature and violent death.

The one they had come to see as the "promised one," the mighty prophet and messiah, the one who offered to them and to their nation sovereignty and freedom, has been snatched from their view. With his death, they are downcast in hopelessness and dejection.

Unable to see beyond the event of his death, they are entombed by their own interior blindness. Stunned by his crucifixion and death, their vision has narrowed and seemingly occludes all confidence in their dreams for the future. They are locked in doubt!

Yet, the travelers are still discussing the painful event as if some small remnant of saving vision might surface. Into this fragile, dismembered, yet still flickering, hope, Jesus enters. He sensitively draws out the greater wisdom held bound within their own hearts.

Their vision dulled, they see Jesus as a stranger. His leading questions stir and agitate them. Jesus patiently listens as they relive their anguish and loss.

With unerring accuracy, he pinpoints and articulates for them their greatest blind spot of unbelief. They have failed to grasp the value and role of suffering.

They do not recognize Jesus.

In their grief they have neglected their own scriptural heritage, which saw in suffering love the way to the restoration of sight to the blind and freedom to those imprisoned (Isa. 53:10; 61:1,2).

With Jesus, they relive in memory the everlasting faithfulness of the God of the Passover, who led their ancestors from exile to promise, from death to life. In remembering, their hope is reawakened. The story of their people is once again their own; their hearts are opened to receive the fullness of God's promise.

What in the morning had seemed like bad news, now, by evening, has taken on a different light.

"Stay with us."

Jesus enters their lodging. He who on the way had seemed a stranger allows himself to be seen and known by them. The one who had been invited as a guest becomes for them the host (Jer. 18:4–9).

Jesus takes bread, blesses it, breaks it, and gives it to them. Through his word and action, their entire life—all they have known and all that is to come—is held and made holy.

They know him! In the moment of recognition he vanishes. His presence with them is no longer dependent on his physical person. On the road and at the table he has gifted them with a deeper sense of his presence.

Their life, once reduced to loss, has now become a leaven of hope and light for a world shrouded in shadow.

The *only* news is the good news of Jesus Christ. He is risen!

Suggested Approach to Prayer: On the Way

+ *Daily prayer pattern:* (See pages 1 and 2.)
I quiet myself and relax in the presence of God.
I declare my dependency on God.

+ *Grace:* I ask to share in the joy of Jesus, risen.

+ *Method:* Meditation, as on page 3.
One morning two people found themselves on a journey. I reread Luke 24:13–35. It is my journey, too:
"Two of them were on their way . . . talking together about all that had happened."
  • I review the life events, feelings, and hopes of my recent past.
"Their eyes were prevented from recognising him."
  • Where have I most experienced a blurring of inner vision of the Risen Jesus?
"'What are all these things that you are discussing . . . ?'"
  • What questions, what concerns have been rising into my consciousness?
"Going through all the prophets, he explained to them . . . the scriptures . . . ."
  • What scriptural passages have most deeply called and supported me?
"'Was it not necessary that the Christ should suffer before entering into his glory?'"
  • Where have I most experienced suffering leading into joy?
"They pressed him to stay with them . . . ."
  • Who and what are the strangers I have invited into the circle of my life?
"They . . . recognized him at the breaking of bread."
  • Where, when, and how have I most met and recognized Christ?
"They set out that instant and returned to Jerusalem."
  • How will I share the good news that Jesus lives?

+ *Closing:* I enter into conversation with Christ, letting my heart speak simply, lovingly, passionately to him. I pray the Our Father.

+ *Review of prayer:* In my journal I note any insights and feelings that have surfaced during my prayer.

Week 2, Day 6: Repetition

Suggested Approach to Prayer

+ *Daily prayer pattern:* (See pages 1 and 2.)
I quiet myself and relax in the presence of God.
I declare my dependency on God.

+ *Grace:* I ask for a deep sharing in the joy of the Risen Christ.

+ *Method:* Repetition, as on page 6.

In preparation, I review my prayer periods by reading my journal of the past week. I select for repetition the period of prayer in which I was most deeply moved or one in which I experienced a lack of emotional response or one in which I was grasped with insight or one in which I experienced confusion. I use the method with which I approached the passage initially. I open myself to hear again God's word to me in that particular passage.

+ *Review of prayer:* In my journal, I write any feelings, experiences, or insights that have surfaced in this second listening.

Week 3, Day 1: Easter Tidings for the Twenty-first Century

ISA. 35:1–10

Let the desert and the dry lands be glad,
let the wasteland rejoice and bloom;
like the asphodel, let it burst into flower,
let it rejoice and sing for joy.
The glory of Lebanon is bestowed on it,
the splendour of Carmel and Sharon;
then they will see the glory of Yahweh,
the splendour of our God.
Strengthen all weary hands,
steady all trembling knees
and say to the faint-hearted,
"Be strong! Do not be afraid.
Here is your God,
vengeance is coming,
divine retribution;
he is coming to save you."

Then the eyes of the blind will be opened,
the ears of the deaf unsealed,
then the lame will leap like a deer
and the tongue of the dumb sing for joy;
for water will gush in the desert
and streams in the wasteland,
the parched ground will become a marsh
and the thirsty land springs of water;
the lairs where the jackals used to live
will become plots of reed and papyrus.

And through it will run a road for them and a
            highway
which will be called the Sacred Way;
the unclean will not be allowed to use it;
He will be the one to use this road,
the fool will not stray along it.
No lion will be there,
no ferocious beast set foot on it,
nothing of the sort be found;
it will be used by the redeemed.
For those whom Yahweh has ransomed will return,
they will come to Zion shouting for joy,
their heads crowned with joy unending;
rejoicing and gladness will escort them
and sorrow and sighing will take flight.

To People of the Twenty-first Century

Listen!
Let the saddened and despaired lift their eyes;
Let those whose hearts are heavy breathe freely.
Let them birth forth new children in hope;
            and care for their young in promise.

A new age is opening before us,
            an age of oneness and peace,
where we shall see in each other
            a new vision fresh as a first moment.

Tell all you know to take courage
            to claim inner power and strength.
There is no need to be overwhelmed or to fear;
            darkness is but prelude to dawn.

The drugged and addicted will awaken
        with integrity where idols fall.
Limbs paralyzed with indecision and fear
        will now walk unencumbered and free.
Rejoice!
The poor will be poor no longer;
        the rich will be rich in deed.
And for those who wander our streets, weary:
        the misfortuned will be nourished,
        the elderly and the lost, received.
No longer
        will neighborhoods be wary and armed
        Nor leaders vigilant with mistrust.
No longer
        will resources be burdened with war
        and our youth conditioned to violence.
A new age is upon us;
A new way unfolding
        —beyond détente, beyond force—
Forgiveness will crumble walls;
        trust become the builder of cities.
Reverence will be the blessing
        embracing our entire planet.
Never, never war in the stars!
        Magi satellites will network a communion and message of love.
Rejoice!
The earth will be renewed.
As ancient redwoods stand in surety,
        And quakes are gentled by prayer.
Then land, once shackled and dormant with mortgage,
        will sevenfold yield its abundance.

The earth will be renewed!

Pure water for the many: fresh, clean
        nourishing life deep within.

All deserts, wastelands watered,
        all thirsty fires quenched.

The earth will be renewed and live!

Dare to dream; creation is upon us.
        Death's door has been slammed shut.

The end, though forecast as doom,
        is—oh, joy—joy!

Listen! Jesus is come, risen, alive.
        He brings new hope, promises fulfilled.

The path he walked is a highway for us
        Through chaos and ashes, his Spirit leads.

Suggested Approach to Prayer: Prayer of Renewal

+ *Daily prayer pattern:* (See pages 1 and 2.)
I quiet myself and relax in the presence of God.
I declare my dependency on God.

+ *Grace:* I ask for a share in the joy of Jesus, risen.

+ *Method:* Meditative reading, as on page 5.
Aware of the presence of the Spirit of the Risen Jesus, I prayerfully and slowly read "Easter Tidings for the Twenty-first Century."

As I make my way through the message, I allow myself to be open to the awareness that Christ, risen, is active throughout the world, bringing about the healing and joy of the tidings.

I pause frequently throughout the message, giving thanks for the presence and power of his Spirit.

I reread Isa. 35:1–10 and "To People of the Twenty-first Century."

I am aware that the Spirit of Christ is within me, inviting and empowering me to use whatever gifts I have to participate in the world's renewal.

Slowly I again read the scriptural passage from Isaiah and "To People of the Twenty-first Century." As images surface before me, I pray the presence of the Risen Christ within them, for example, I pray for the depressed to receive hope, for the addicted to receive strength, for the bound to gain freedom, for the earth to receive regeneration.

+ *Closing:* I enter into a conversation with the Risen Christ, sharing with him my gratitude and joy. I pray the Our Father.

+ *Review of prayer:* I note in my journal whatever feelings or insights have surfaced during my prayer.

Week 3, Day 2: The Center of Centers

1 COR. 4:7

Has anybody given you some special right? What do you have that was not given to you? And if it was given, how can you boast as though it were not?

The center of all centers is God.

To be dynamic, every living organism needs a center that provides stability and direction. The need for a center is evident in every sector of life—physical, biological, psychological, social, and cultural.

Our planet earth as part of the solar system has as its center the sun. This center serves as the energy source for the harmonious integration of all the earth's cycles and the rhythms of nature.

A "living system *par excellence*" (24, p. 292) is the brain, the structurally complex center of the human body. With its vastly intricate synapses, relays, and reflexes, the brain assumes the role of maintaining a state of optimum activity for the entire human organism.

As the center of all centers, God is the integrating force, the fire, and the essence of reality, bringing together all elements of being into the amazing mystery we call life.

Just as the earth would fall into darkness without the sun or as the human body would die without its brain, so too without God as our center life becomes empty and meaningless, a lonely journey to nowhere. If God is not our center, our life consists merely of a desperate and frantic clutching in order to gratify the deep needs within.

Where God is not Lord, possessiveness and pride lay claim. To be in touch with God as the center and source of everything is to recognize that all is gift. From this authentic perspective there is little or no temptation toward puffed-up smugness. Spiritual poverty does not leave room for competitive wrangling and destructive judgmentalism.

God is the giver; whatever anyone has, material or spiritual, comes from God. God alone is the judge of the gift and the gifted.

"What have you got that was not given to you?"

Everything is gift, and all of life is thanksgiving!

Suggested Approach to Prayer: Love—God's Gifts

+ *Daily prayer pattern:* (See pages 1 and 2.)
I quiet myself and relax in the presence of God.
I declare my dependency on God.

+ *Grace:* I ask for the gift of a sensitive and intimate knowledge of God's goodness to me in order that, filled with thanksgiving, I may be empowered to respond totally in my love and service to God.

+ *Method:* Contemplation, as on page 3.
When contemplating God's love, I hold before me two important points regarding love:
   • Authentic love expresses itself in deeds over and above words.
   • Love consists in a mutual sharing between those who love each other.
With these truths held in my heart, I consider God's gifts to me. I remember how I was conceived and born and how I have been baptized and confirmed.

I consider how the Creator's gift of God's self to me has been total. I recall how, at each moment, God continues to gift me with the fullness of creation.

In God's love, I continue to be born and blessed daily, even moment by moment.

I affectionately recall the many blessings and gifts God has so generously lavished upon me.

I remember the ways God's love has particularly touched *me,* choosing me to exist among the myriad possibilities, gifting me with my own uniqueness.

"'If you only knew what God is offering'" (John 4:10).
   • If only I could realize the fullness of the special gift of myself, all that I am—my body, my faculties of intellect, will, imagination, memory, and emotions . . . I ponder and rejoice . . .

- If only I could realize the fullness of the gift that relationships with others bring me . . . I ponder and rejoice . . .
- If only I could realize the fullness of the gift of the beauty and sustaining force of nature . . . I ponder and rejoice . . .
- If only I could realize the fullness of the healing and transforming spiritual gifts that are available to me through God's Son and the community of believers . . . I ponder and rejoice.

"What have you got that was not given to you?"

To such a fullness of love given, I desire to respond with the fullness of myself. I pray:

Take, Lord, and receive all my liberty, my memory, my understanding, and my entire will—all that I have and call my own. You have given it all to me. To you, Lord, I return it. Everything is yours; do with it what you will. Give me only your love and your grace. That is enough for me (43, p. 141).

+ *Review of prayer:* In my journal I take note of feelings and insights that have surfaced during my prayer.

Week 3, Day 3: The Face of Love

1 JOHN 4:7–19

My dear friends,
let us love each other
since love is from God
and everyone who loves is a child of God and
            knows God.
Whoever fails to love does not know God,
because God is love.
This is the revelation of God's love for us,
that God sent his only Son into the world
that we might have life through him.
Love consists in this;
it is not we who loved God,
but God loved us and sent his Son
to expiate our sins.
My dear friends,
if God loved us so much,
we too should love each other.
No one has ever seen God,
but as long as we love each other
God remains in us
and his love comes to its perfection in us.
This is the proof that we remain in him
and he in us,
that he has given us a share in his Spirit.
We ourselves have seen and testify
that the Father sent his Son
as Saviour of the world.

Anyone who acknowledges that Jesus is the Son
of God,
God remains in him and he in God.
We have recognised for ourselves,
and put our faith in, the love God has for us.
God is love,
and whoever remains in love remains in God
and God in him.
Love comes to its perfection in us
when we can face the Day of Judgement fearlessly,
because even in this world
we have become as he is.
In love there is no room for fear,
but perfect love drives out fear,
because fear implies punishment
and whoever is afraid has not come to perfection
in love.
Let us love, then,
because he first loved us.

When, in *The Divine Comedy*, the medieval poet Dante passed through hell and purgatory and reached the pinnacle of heaven, he came face to face with the mystery that grounds all reality, "the love that moved the sun and other stars" (74, canto 33, line 146). In comparison to this love, all else paled: sight failed, dreams faded, snow melted! Dante was before the living light (1 John 4:10).

His own sight failing, Dante saw a new vision of wholeness, totally unparalleled. His intellect, though keen, surrendered before the incomprehensible. Dante was swept into the vision; his will was drawn precipitately into the blinding knowledge of the illumination. In obedience to his deepest being, Dante plunged into the perfect rest and rhythm of the power and peace of the eternal, ever new, reality of God's love. Dante was never again the same (1 John 4:16).

Touched deeply by the healing and creative light of his experience, Dante mysteriously became the vision of his desire (1 John 4:17).

At the end of his transforming journey, Dante gifted the ages with the exquisite witness,

Rolling like a wheel that never jars,
my will and wish were now by love impelled,
the love that moves the Sun and th' other stars.
                    (74, canto 33, lines 145–146)

Dante had tasted heaven! The vision that unfolded before him was that of love. The incredible gift of Dante's witness is the inspiration we receive to set out courageously and to fully claim the unique treasure of love's potential awaiting within each of us.

The desire to *see God* is and will always be the greatest, the most unyielding élan of the human heart. Like Dante's, our limited human powers are not able to satisfy our innate longings for God. Our greatest power, like his, lies in our surrender to the One who alone is the power (1 John 4:16). This power is love; God is love (ibid., 4:8).

Dante, transfixed by the light of his vision, sees within it the human face of Christ, God's Word of love become human.

Through the words and actions of Christ, through his birth, life, death, and resurrection, God's love has taken on human expression. In the human face of Christ, all those who believe *see* the contours of God's love (ibid., 4:11–12).

The marvel continues even further; in the words and actions of those who "see" Christ, God is seen, again made flesh (ibid., 4:9).

As Christ is Son of God, so too we are sons and daughters of God, begotten and held in the embrace of love. In the light of such joy and confidence, fear loses its power and can have no secure hold (ibid., 4:18).

The voice of love impels us forward to the perfect love's goal, the creation of a community of love whose many members, like unique facets, reveal the magnitude and graciousness of God who is love (ibid., 4:19).

Where God is seen as love, Christmas happens every day, and Easter never ceases. Life thus fully lived, fully dared, is a "Dante" experience, a "divine comedy" where to see is to love and to love is to live forever (ibid., 4:13).

Suggested Approach to Prayer: Proclamation of Love

+ *Daily prayer pattern:* (See pages 1 and 2.)
I quiet myself and relax in the presence of God.
I declare my dependency on God.

+ *Grace:* I ask for the gift of a sensitive and intimate knowledge of God's goodness to me, in order that, filled with thanksgiving, I may be empowered to respond totally in my love and service to God.

+ *Method:* Meditative reading, as on page 5.
I review the previous exercise of prayer.
Recalling the uniqueness and totalness of God's love for me, I meditatively read John's proclamation of God's love, 1 John 4:7–19.
I read slowly, pausing periodically, allowing the words and phrases to enter into me. When a thought or a feeling resonates deeply, I stay with it, allowing the fullness of it to penetrate my being.
I savor the word; I respond authentically and spontaneously as in a dialogue.

+ *Closing:* I pray:
Take, Lord, and receive all my liberty, my memory, my understanding, and my entire will—all that I have and call my own. You have given it all to me. To you, Lord, I return it. Everything is yours; do with it what you will. Give me only your love and your grace. That is enough for me (43, p. 141).

+ *Review of prayer:* In my journal I note feelings and insights that have surfaced during my prayer.

Week 3, Day 4: Through Locked Doors

JOHN 20:19-23

In the evening of that same day, the first day of the week, the doors were closed in the room where the disciples were, for fear of the Jews. Jesus came and stood among them. He said to them, "Peace be with you," and, after saying this, he showed them his hands and his side. The disciples were filled with joy at seeing the Lord, and he said to them again, "Peace be with you.

> *"As the Father sent me,*
> *so am I sending you."*

After saying this he breathed on them and said:

> *Receive the Holy Spirit.*
> *If you forgive anyone's sins,*
> *they are forgiven;*
> *if you retain anyone's sins,*
> *they are retained.*

On such a tree my spirit crouched,
Deluded by its powerlessness,
Till seeing with joy how great its Lord,
It found from sorrow swift release.
(54, *Upanishads*, p. 56)

When Christ died on the tree of the cross, all the hopes and dreams of the disciples were shattered. Their courageous zeal yielded to fear and listlessness. Their confidence gave way to disbelief and doubt. Locked, indeed, into their own powerlessness, the disciples were dispirited. It was as if when Jesus died they lost their soul.

Where had it all gone? What had happened to the magnanimity that had filled their spirit when Jesus first called them? In companionship with him their life had been enlarged and filled with purpose. Now they were imprisoned by confusion and grief.

"Peace be with you."

Jesus enters through the locked door of the disciples' hearts. He pierces their fear and seizes hold of them. In his presence the walls of their confinement tumble.

This is Jesus of Nazareth! He stands before them, risen in power yet bearing his wounds.

Transfixed by his risen presence, the disciples are delivered into enthralling, ecstatic joy!

He had promised his beloved disciples at their last meal together that he would return. He had promised that he would bring them a peace that would heal and strengthen them beyond their most cherished dreams (John 14:27ff.). Now he is before them.

"Peace be with you."

The moment when the disciples were given birth has now suddenly come to fullness (John 3:5-6). Through the breath of Christ, they receive the life and power of the Spirit. The new creation has begun (Gen. 2:7ff.)!

Having breathed of the same Spirit, the disciples are one with each other and with Christ, brothers and sisters in him. All members of the community share with Christ his mission of reconciliation and peace.

The entire community is empowered and sent to bring to others Christ's spirit of unconditional love and forgiveness.

Filled with fresh excitement and urgency of purpose, the disciples' spirits are flushed with the rich prophetic breath of God, *ruah-Yahweh*, that flows through their ancestral past. Yahweh says, "'I am now going to make the breath enter you, and you will live'" (Ezek. 37:5).

The promise of the ages has come to fulfillment! In the Spirit of Jesus, the word of Yahweh is sorrow's sweet release (Rev. 21:4)!

Suggested Approach to Prayer: The Breath of Christ

+ *Daily prayer pattern:* (See pages 1 and 2).
  I quiet myself and relax in the presence of God.
  I declare my dependency on God.

+ *Grace:* I ask to share in the joy of the Risen Christ.

+ *Method:* Contemplation, as on page 3.

I form a mental image of myself in a room with locked doors. It is evening.

I take note of the other people in the room with me—who they are, their facial expressions, the comments they are making to each other.

I consider the reasons that we have locked ourselves in the room. I am aware of the fear I see in the other people, and I ask myself what it is within me that has me locked in. I ask myself, is it fear, guilt, shame, self-doubt . . . ?

Suddenly Jesus is present. I form an image of him standing before me, his wounds visible. I consider how he has passed through the locked door of the room, the locked door of my heart.

I hear his words, "Peace be with you."

I allow the words to be absorbed deeply within me.

Looking at Jesus, I see compassion and love in his eyes. He breathes on us; I experience his breath descend upon me.

I breathe in deeply the breath of Christ. I allow the breath to enter through my nostrils, move down into my lungs and through my body.

As I exhale, all my negativity is released. I feel my anger, doubt, fear, and so on, like so much dust, released into the air.

I continue in this manner, breathing in the breath of the Spirit of Christ, breathing out negativity. As I continue to breathe in and out, I experience the heaviness leave me until gradually I feel lighter. I feel loved and forgiven. I rest in the freedom of being forgiven.

I visualize before me those people who have hurt me, who have caused me pain. Filled now with the Spirit of Christ's forgiving love, I breathe on each one in turn, allowing the unconditional love present in my heart to descend on each of them. I continue forgiving each one until my heart is released from its imprisonment.

I experience the inner harmony and freedom of the gift of the peace of Christ. I hear the voice of Christ say, "Peace be with you."

+ *Closing:* I allow my heart to respond personally and intimately to Christ. I pray the Our Father.

+ *Review of prayer:* I note in my journal the insights and feelings that have surfaced during my prayer.

Week 3, Day 5: Enduring Fragrance

2 COR. 2:14–16

Thanks be to God who always gives us in Christ a part in his triumphal procession, and through us is spreading everywhere the fragrance of the knowledge of himself. To God we are the fragrance of Christ, both among those who are being saved and among those who are on the way to destruction; for these last, the smell of death leading to death, but for the first, the smell of life leading to life.

A son says to his mother, "I always know when you're home because I smell your perfume the moment I come through the door."

The scent of her fragrance carries the mother's presence. For her son, the fragrance of her loving memory will always be a source of nurturance, comfort, and joy. The fragrance of her love will continue throughout his life to sensitize and enable him to recognize the presence of "the smell of life leading to life."

Only in being loved and in loving others is this fragrance of love released. This most precious of all fragrances is called joy.

God is the essence of all love, and joy is the natural fragrance of all people who are in touch with the nurturing presence of God's motherhood in their life.

Jesus is the ultimate human expression of God's love. He is God's redolent presence among us (Matt. 1:23).

The birthing of Christ, God's own Son, is for all of creation the lavish outpouring of God's love. Christ's Spirit, risen, fills the entire world with joy. Unrestrainable, this fragrance diffuses itself to all who come within its ambience.

Joy is at once apparent and transparent, permeating the entire spirit of those who have entered into intimacy with Christ.

The joy of Christ is an active, powerful force in the life of all who are gifted with it. It creates, heals, envisions, unifies. Through the gift of joy, our will becomes resilient and responsive to God's will and intent. All our decisions and works are grounded with a spiritual instinct that guides us firmly in the path of Christ.

Our life is lived in freedom and confidence and becomes for others the fragrance of Christ.

Through the joy of the Risen Christ, the people of God are consecrated. They are anointed with his Spirit, the "oil of gladness" (Heb. 1:9), and become a celebration of Christ's presence in the world.

Suggested Approach to Prayer: Oil of Gladness

+ *Daily prayer pattern:* (See pages 1 and 2).
  I quiet myself and relax in the presence of God.
  I declare my dependency on God.

+ *Grace:* I ask to share in the joy of the Risen Christ.

+ *Method:* Contemplation, as on page 3.
"Be thy hands anointed with holy oil, be thy breast anointed with holy oil, be thy head anointed with holy oil, as kings, priests, prophets were anointed." These were the words proclaimed by the archbishop of Canterbury as, beneath the golden canopy, Elizabeth II was anointed during her coronation, 2 June 1953 (58, p. 161).

The ancient ritual of anointing is considered the most significant feature of the coronation solemnity of kings and queens. By virtue of the anointing, the sovereign is consecrated for a sacred purpose. This holy ritual is derived from the anointing of kings, prophets, and priests as recorded in the Jewish Scriptures.

Through the anointing with oil, the aura of power that accompanies prophecy and priestliness is bestowed on the royalty.

Traditionally, oil has been regarded as a sign of the outpouring of the healing, strengthening, consoling presence of God. At the anointing of Queen Elizabeth II, a secret formula was used for the preparation of the precious oils and exquisite perfumes. The amber-colored unguent included "the oils of orange flowers, or roses, cinnamon, jasmine, and sesame with benzoin, musk, civet and ambergris" (76, p. 339). The hope and promise enlivened in her people at Elizabeth's ascent to the throne was captured in the fragrant beauty of the chrism. For the people of the United Kingdom, the oil of Elizabeth's anointing was an oil of gladness.

At the inauguration of his ministry at the synagogue in Nazareth, Jesus claimed his own anointing.

The spirit of the Lord is on me,
for he has anointed me
to bring the good news to the afflicted.
He has sent me to proclaim liberty to captives,
sight to the blind,
to let the oppressed go free,
to proclaim a year of favour from the Lord.

(Luke 4:18–19)

Through the Spirit, Jesus was anointed into a prophetic, priestly, royal servanthood.

I envision myself standing beneath a golden canopy of anointing. I wait, with expectation, the confirming action of the Spirit.

As I am anointed, I breathe deeply of the fragrant oil, allowing its bouquet to refresh my soul.

As the oil touches my skin, I experience its soothing and healing essence. I take pleasure in the oil as it penetrates and relieves the dryness of my body.

Relaxing totally in the ambience of the sacred oil, I allow God's healing and guiding Spirit to be absorbed deeply within my being.

As my head is anointed, I pray, "Lord God, may your Spirit instill me with wisdom and direction of life that is according to your will for me. Release my mind from any strongholds or obstacles that are contrary to your Spirit. Lord, I beg that my mind will be set free to obey Christ always and in all things."

I rest gently in the sacredness of this moment as I hear the words, "Be thy head anointed with holy oil, as kings, priests, prophets were anointed."

As my heart is anointed, I pray, "Lord God, may your Spirit gift me with a profound sense of being held within the embrace of your unconditional love. Heal my heart of the woundedness that inhibits my capacity to give and to receive love. Lord, I beg that my heart will be totally immersed in the healing love of God's Spirit and set free in gladness."

I rest gently in the sacredness of this moment as I hear the words, "Be thy heart anointed with holy oil, as kings, priests, prophets were anointed."

As my hands are anointed, I pray, "Lord God, may your Spirit empower me that I might bring to the world a service of reconciliation and peace. Rescue me from the fears that tend to propel me into isolation, withdrawal, and passivity. Release me, O Lord, from all grasping and possessiveness so that my hands might be opened totally to using my gifts in loving service to others."

I rest gently in the sacredness of this moment as I hear the words, "Be thy hands anointed with holy oil, as kings, priests, prophets were anointed."

+ *Closing:* I conclude my prayer by giving thanks for the anointing of the Spirit that is my royal inheritance as a son or daughter of God and follower of Christ. I pray the Our Father.

+ *Review of prayer:* I write in my journal the insights and feelings that have surfaced during my prayer.

Week 3, Day 6: Repetition

Suggested Approach to Prayer

+ *Daily prayer pattern:* (See pages 1 and 2.)
  I quiet myself and relax in the presence of God.
  I declare my dependency on God.

+ *Grace:* I ask for a deep sharing in the joy of the Risen Christ.

+ *Method:* Repetition, as on page 6.
  In preparation, I review my prayer periods by reading my journal of the past week. I select for repetition the period of prayer in which I was most deeply moved or one in which I experienced a lack of emotional response or one in which I was grasped with insight or one in which I experienced confusion. I use the method with which I approached the passage initially. I open myself to hear again God's word to me in that particular passage.

+ *Review of prayer:* In my journal, I write any feelings, experiences, or insights that have surfaced in this second listening.

Peace
be with
you.
LK 24:36

Week 4, Day 1: Through a Closed Door

JOHN 20:24–29

Thomas, called the Twin, who was one of the Twelve, was not with them when Jesus came. So the other disciples said to him, "We have seen the Lord," but he answered, "Unless I can see the holes that the nails made in his hands and can put my finger into the holes they made, and unless I can put my hand into his side, I refuse to believe." Eight days later the disciples were in the house again and Thomas was with them. The doors were closed, but Jesus came in and stood among them. "Peace be with you," he said. Then he spoke to Thomas, "Put your finger here; look, here are my hands. Give me your hand; put it into my side. Do not be unbelieving anymore but believe." Thomas replied, "My Lord and my God!" Jesus said to him:

> *You believe because you can see me.*
> *Blessed are those who have not seen and yet believe.*

Are you enjoying the taste and delight of Easter, or are you still waiting for the Easter egg hunt to get under way?

We proudly lay claim to being an Easter people, yet how often we fail to savor the Easter mystery within our heart or to nourish its joy in our family and community.

Are we, like Thomas, out of step with Easter?

At times, we, too, find ourselves locked in doubt, sadly refusing joy's entry into our life. This locked-in-ness is a subtle phenomenon, a gradual giving way to insecurities and self-doubt from which springs a fundamental demand for proofs and miraculous intervention.

We put on blinders and say, "Show me!"

Whatever barriers to openness our circumstances or world may construct, they are definitively surpassed by the ultimate energy of Easter. The power and vision of Easter unfailingly penetrate our doubt, however bolted and secure its entrenchment may be.

This great and unrivaled energy of Easter paradoxically gains its entry through the gentle presence of the Risen Christ. It was into the midst of the anguish and loneliness of doubt that Christ suddenly appeared to Thomas. It is in the midst of our woundedness that Christ continues to be a healing Easter presence.

Amazingly, it was the blinding doubt of Thomas that served the function of making known to the world the wonder of God's merciful love. His skeptical bargaining was met with unconditional acceptance by Jesus. Jesus did not rebuke Thomas. He accepted him totally, going so far as to invite him to satisfy his appetite for proof by putting his hand into the wound in his side, his finger into the wounds of his hands and feet.

Thomas's heart was instantly overwhelmed with the awareness of the magnitude of Christ's gentleness and understanding. Pierced through with such love, Thomas *knew;* he knew with the knowledge of the Spirit.

"My Lord and my God!"

He knew that it was Jesus crucified and risen. Thomas saw with a more penetrating vision, with his inner eye.

"My Lord and my God!"

In his act of surrender, the wounds of doubt, like agonizing boils, are first pierced then healed by Jesus' love. Thomas became whole in the strength of conviction and commitment. Once again power was made perfect in weakness (2 Cor. 12:9).

In the gentleness of the moment, the history of all previous generations met the promise of the New Age. Jesus' concluding words assure happiness to those who believe without seeing. In that promise, we intuit Christ's predilection for those of us who, as members of his new-age Easter community, are sustained by his empowering word and the abiding presence of his Spirit.

The experience of Thomas ushered in a new era of belief and hope.

Joy has entered! Easter is now!

Into the future the Spirit of the Risen Christ will guide the vision of the Easter community. In a world wounded and scarred, the followers of Jesus reach through and beyond the pain to see the sacred stigmata of Christ, risen and healing.

Suggested Approach to Prayer: The Easter Wish (first exercise)

+ *Daily prayer pattern:* (See pages 1 and 2.)
  I quiet myself and relax in the presence of God.
  I declare my dependency on God.

+ *Grace:* I ask to share in the joy of the Risen Christ.

+ *Preparation Before Prayer*
  We are sincere in our desire to live out fully the potential of the Easter promise that dwells within us. Our world as well as our personal history and behavioral patterning makes this difficult. Like Thomas, we frequently succumb to the insidious and subtle pitfalls of doubt.

  We are, however, far from being at the mercy of the circumstances that militate against our progress and our joy. We have the creative energy of the Spirit. This Spirit gives strength to our deep desire to live in the manner of Jesus. It is the motivating force and healing energy that transforms our wounds into our greatest gifts.

  We are truly able to reach with our inner eye through and beyond our wounds to the Easter dwelling within. It is the call of every Christian woman and man to cooperate with Christ in this labor of transformation.

  In his book, *Unlimited Power,* Anthony Robbins teaches a neurolinguistic approach, amusingly called the "swish," that facilitates this transformation process.

  He asks his clients to construct, in imagination, a large, bright, and detailed image of the behavior they wish to change. Then, in the lower right-hand corner of this large negative image, they are asked to construct a smaller picture that represents themselves as they would desire to be.

  The negative behavior to be changed is then swished through with the most positive behavior. The small positive picture rapidly enlarges, brightens, and bursts through the representation of the undesirable behavior. As the client does this, he or she enthusiastically says the word, "whoosh!" This process is repeated over and over with great rapidity.

The result is that the brain receives a surge of powerful positive signals. Its association patterns are redirected to a more life-giving, positive behavior.

Robbins maintains that consistent perseverance in this technique will bring a person to the point where the inner unresourceful state will itself automatically trigger a parallel resourceful state (92, pp. 86–110).

+ *Prayer Approach*

For the Christian, the ideal resourceful state is the conscious awareness of the presence of the Spirit of the Risen Christ within himself or herself and the way and manner this Spirit is lived out in daily life.

"Let your minds be filled with everything that is true" (Phil. 4:8).

When in our daily experience we find ourselves, like Thomas, behind a closed door, that is, in an unresourceful state of doubt, we can call on the Easter power within us to alter our consciousness into one of confident resourcefulness and joy.

Prayerfully adapting the practical and innovative approach of Robbins, I proceed.

With my inner eye, I see my wounded self in a state of doubt. I see myself at a time when I lose sight of the presence and power of Christ's Spirit within me.

Clearly and concretely and in great detail, I see the negative image of my behavior at this time. I see it represented in a large and bright manner.

Using the following questions, I relax and bring the image of myself in a state of doubt into as sharp a focus as possible:

- What does my posture look like?
- How do I walk?
- How do I hold my head?
- What is the volume, rhythm, tone, and timbre of my voice?
- What is the dominant message I am saying to myself?
- Do I feel this image as soft or firm, rigid or flexible . . . ?
- If I were to taste this image, would it be sour or sweet or bitter?
- What colors predominate, or is this image in blacks, whites, grays?
- Is it near or at a distance? Do I see it as an outsider viewing it from a distance, or do I look at it with my own eyes?

- Is my image contained as in a frame, or is it frameless, extending indefinitely?

When I have before me a clear representation of how I experience my state of doubting, I proceed to create in the lower right-hand corner of this representation a darker and smaller picture of myself in a resourceful state, that is, as I would be if I made the desired change.

Using the questions listed above, I develop a distinct, clear image of what I want. I see this picture grow in size, brightness, and volume. I take the picture and hurl it through the previous image, through the behavior I no longer desire. I propel the positive image through the negative image rapidly, like a sun bursting through and disintegrating the negative behavior. As I do this, I say the word "whoosh!" with all the enthusiasm I can muster. The goal is to feel and see the previously small image of positive behavior replacing the initially large image with an even bigger, brighter image of myself as I desire to be.

I allow myself to feel the wonderful delight of being who and what I most deeply want to be, the beautiful person God has created me to be. Then I open my eyes briefly to interrupt the imaging.

I close my eyes again and repeat this "swish." Again, I start by seeing the large image of what I want to change, and then I see the small image grow brighter and pass through it. I pause, allow myself to feel it, open my eyes. Again I close my eyes and repeat the "swish," as quickly as possible, five or six more times.

I allow myself to enjoy this whole process (92, pp. 86–110).

Happy with the new vision of myself as more Christlike, I unite myself with Thomas in acclaiming, "My Lord and my God!"

+ *Closing:* I conclude my prayer with a conversation with Christ, letting my heart speak of my deep desire and gratitude. I pray the Our Father.

+ *Review of prayer:* I write in my journal whatever in my prayer period will be helpful in using this approach in the future.

Week 4, Day 2: In Laughter and Tears

PHIL. 4:4–9

Always be joyful, then, in the Lord; I repeat, be joyful. Let your good sense be obvious to everybody. The Lord is near. Never worry about anything; but tell God all your desires of every kind in prayer and petition shot through with gratitude, and the peace of God which is beyond our understanding will guard your hearts and your thoughts in Christ Jesus. Finally, brothers, let your minds be filled with everything that is true, everything that is honourable, everything that is upright and pure, everything that we love and admire—with whatever is good and praiseworthy. Keep doing everything you learnt from me and were told by me and have heard or seen me doing. Then the God of peace will be with you.

As this children's song reflects, God laughs in the laughter of children; God sings in their heart.

The spontaneous and totally free laughter of children captures the essence of happiness that God wants for all children. The fact that we have grown tall and have become what is commonly known as mature should not serve to stifle our spontaneity and joy.

Even though, as adults, we are subject to the many faces of hostility and breakdown that characterize society, our joy in life can be constant. Our happiness is not contingent on the presence of perfection or the absence of pain.

In other words, we need not wait for heaven to sing the alleluia. The Easter Christ is here; "'the season of glad songs has come'" (Song of Songs 2:12).

Easter is a mystery like the mystery of pregnancy; it is fullness *and* waiting. Our heart is filled with Easter yet poised in eager expectation of Christ's coming in the fullness of time, the Omega.

"Rejoice," says Paul to the Christian community. "Sing psalms and hymns and inspired songs to God" (Col. 3:16).

Feeling alienated in a world taut with anguish and suffering, it becomes difficult for us not to echo the grieving of the exiled people of the Jewish Scriptures, "How could we sing a song of Yahweh / on alien soil?" (Ps. 137:4).

As people of the new creation, we look to the words and example of Jesus for our strength and perseverance. Christ's willing embrace of suffering with his subsequent rise to glory is the confirming sign and promise that pain is not an obstacle to happiness. His words reassure us, "You will be sorrowful, / but your sorrow will turn to joy" (John 16:20).

In Christ, God is ever near.

In a touching incident in the life of Peter Abelard, God's poignant and tender nearness is brought home to us.

Peter and his companion, Thibault, heard in the woods a piercing scream like the cry of a child in great pain. They found a small rabbit caught in a trap. As they freed it, the rabbit nuzzled into Peter's arms and died.

"It was that last confiding thrust that broke Abelard's heart . . . 'Thibault,' he said, 'do you think there is a God at all? Whatever has come to me, I earned it. But what did this one do?' Thibault nodded. 'I know,' he said. 'Only—I think God is in it too.' Abelard looked up sharply. 'In it? Do you mean that it makes Him suffer the way it does us?' Again Thibault nodded . . . 'All this,' he stroked the limp body, 'is because of us. But all the time God suffers. More than we do.' Abelard looked at him, perplexed . . . 'Thibault, do you mean Calvary?' Thibault shook his head. 'That was only a piece of it—the piece that we saw—in time. Like that.' He pointed to a fallen tree beside them, sawn through the middle. 'That dark ring there, it goes up and down the whole length of the tree. But you only see it where it is cut across. That is what Christ's life was; the bit of God that we saw. And we think God is like that, because Christ was like that, kind, and forgiving sins, and healing people. We think God is like that for ever, because it happened once, with Christ. But not the pain. Not the agony at the last. We think that stopped.' Abelard looked at him . . . 'Then, Thibault,' he said slowly, 'you think that all this . . . all the pain of the world, was Christ's cross?' 'God's cross,' said Thibault. 'And it goes on.' 'The Patripassian heresy,' muttered Abelard mechanically. 'But, oh God, if it were true. Thibault, it must be. At least, there is something at the back of it that is true. And if we could find it—it would bring back the whole world.'" (108, pp. 62–63).

Held in the rhythm of joy and sadness we are an Easter people. In Christ, God is very near. God not only laughs in our laughter; God cries in our tears. To be in the presence of God is to be in joy.

Suggested Approach to Prayer: The Easter Wish (second exercise)

+ *Daily prayer pattern:* (See pages 1 and 2.)
I quiet myself and relax in the presence of God.
I declare my dependency on God.

+ *Grace:* I ask to share in the joy of the Risen Christ.

+ *Prayer Approach:* I hear Paul's words, "Be joyful. . . . let your minds be filled . . . with whatever is good." Following his instruction, I reread and allow my heart to absorb his words, "Brothers, let your minds be filled with everything that is true, everything that is honourable, everything that is upright and pure, everything that we love and admire—with whatever is good and praiseworthy" (Phil. 4:8).

I return to the previous day's approach to prayer; I repeat the approach. Again, I relish the joy of visualizing and appropriating myself as I would be if I were to fully live out the Spirit of the Risen Christ dwelling within me.

+ *Review of prayer:* I write in my journal the insights and feelings that have surfaced during the time of prayer.

Week 4, Day 3: Love's Rising

JOHN 21:1–18

Later on, Jesus revealed himself again to the disciples. It was by the Sea of Tiberias, and it happened like this: Simon Peter, Thomas called the Twin, Nathanael from Cana in Galilee, the sons of Zebedee and two more of his disciples were together. Simon Peter said, "I'm going fishing." They replied, "We'll come with you." They went out and got into the boat but caught nothing that night.

When it was already light, there stood Jesus on the shore, though the disciples did not realise that it was Jesus. Jesus called out, "Haven't you caught anything, friends?" And when they answered, "No," he said, "Throw the net out to starboard and you'll find something." So they threw the net out and could not haul it in because of the quantity of fish. The disciple whom Jesus loved said to Peter, "It is the Lord." At these words "It is the Lord," Simon Peter tied his outer garment round him (for he had nothing on) and jumped into the water. The other disciples came on in the boat, towing the net with the fish; they were only about a hundred yards from land.

As soon as they came ashore they saw that there was some bread there and a charcoal fire with fish cooking on it. Jesus said, "Bring some of the fish you have just caught." Simon Peter went aboard and dragged the net ashore, full of big fish, one hundred and fifty-three of them; and in spite of there being so many the net was not broken. Jesus said to them, "Come and have breakfast." None of the disciples was bold enough to ask, "Who are you?"; they knew quite well it was the Lord. Jesus then stepped forward, took the bread and gave it to them, and the same with the fish. This was the third time that Jesus revealed himself to the disciples after rising from the dead.

When they had eaten, Jesus said to Simon Peter, "Simon son of John, do you love me more than these others do?" He answered, "Yes, Lord, you know I love you." Jesus said to him, "Feed my lambs." A second time he said to him, "Simon son of John, do you love me?" He replied, "Yes, Lord, you know I love you." Jesus said to him, "Look after my sheep." Then he said to him a third time, "Simon son of John, do you love me?" Peter was hurt that he asked him a third time, "Do you love me?" and said, "Lord, you know everything; you know I love you." Jesus said to him, "Feed my sheep.

> *In all truth I tell you,*
> *when you were young*
> *you put on your own belt*
> *and walked where you liked;*
> *but when you grow old*
> *you will stretch out your hands,*
> *and somebody else will put a belt round you*
> *and take you where you would rather not go."*

The Pueblos believed that the dawn would not break forth, that the sun would not rise, if they were not there to welcome it. To listen attentively to the underlying message of this ancient teaching is to open ourselves to the value of primitive wisdom, that inner truth that sleeps within us longing for its dawn.

It was in the night that Peter and the disciples went out to sea in search of fish. The confusion and grief they had experienced immediately following Jesus' death caused them to turn aimlessly toward what was most familiar. They fished all night, yet their nets remained empty. Distraught with loss, they awaited the dawn.

Like those who had gone before them, like all those who would come after, their heart yearned for the warmth of the early morning to break through the darkness of the nighttime of their spirit.

Our yearning, itself, is the awakening voice of God, calling our name. It urges us to arise and watch for the light to break forth. It is in the mist of predawn, in the mysterious moment when darkness and light become one, that we as people who wait and watch serve as the dawn's sentry.

The dawn of the resurrection liberates the heart and mind of those who attend to it. This liberation knows no limits of space or time.

Like undulating cosmic music, the light of dawn enters and emerges. Morning comes. The sun illumines the earth with its restoring, healing warmth. Its light, active and free, plays among the earth's shadows, creating ever-changing patterns of newness and joy.

> I have come into the world as light,
> to prevent anyone who believes in me
> from staying in the dark any more.
> (John 12:46)

Those who watch in darkness, who "wait for the LORD" (Isa. 40:31, RSV) are the channels for the light of the universe, the Risen Christ.

Encouraged by the welcoming voice that greets them at dawn, the disciples respond quickly. Without delay they cast their nets to the other side to reap the harvest of the deep. Seeing the abundance of their catch, they recognize Jesus. The miraculous moment removes the veil of bewilderment that had occluded their vision.

"It is the Lord."

Peter, who had eagerly run to the tomb at the first word of Christ's resurrection (John 20:3), now impetuously jumps into the water and swims to shore to embrace the Christ whom he loves. Naked with the vulnerability of having denied his Master at his darkest hour, Peter prepares himself to be reunited with him.

In the light of the early dawn, Jesus invites the disciples to share in the joyous banquet of the new creation. In the intimacy of a simple meal of bread and fish, they find the assurance of his continuing presence among them.

They are gathered together—the same disciples, same shore, same nets, same fishing. Yet all is different! Christ Risen stands before them in his joy! His light and his power is now their own.

From this day forward, their life will be cast into the whole world, to draw in the multitudes who would feast on the celebration of Love's rising. The mission of Christ has become their own.

Peter's authentic humility can serve as a model for the acceptance of our own failure and weakness.

Peter's passionate love of Christ and his willingness to guard and lead the new community can serve as a model for our own unique response to the Spirit's charge.

If we listen and follow the Spirit's guidance, the inner wisdom within us, and nourish ourselves on the healing presence of Christ, the communion of the New Age of light *will,* in us and through us, break forth in joyful promise.

The dawn is now.

We stand on the shore.

Christ says, "Do you love me?"

Suggested Approach to Prayer: Trusting the Light

+ *Daily prayer pattern:* (See pages 1 and 2.)
  I quiet myself and relax in the presence of God.
  I declare my dependency on God.

+ *Grace:* I ask for the gift of sharing in the joy of the Risen Christ.

+ *Method:* Contemplation, as on page 3.

I form a mental image of myself sitting with Christ on the shore of a lake. I envision in great detail our surroundings.

I see the sky of early dawn with its many hues.

I feel the warmth of the morning sun on my skin.

I hear the gentle sounds of the new day, the waves of the sea, the birds...

I see Jesus who is with me. I allow myself to experience his presence as the light of the universe. This light radiates warmth, love, healing, wisdom, power, and joy. I open all the cells of my body to receive this light. I ready my inner being to absorb fully this light.

As if my whole self were a sponge, I experience myself drawing in every possible ray of the light from Christ.

Trusting the light, I give myself permission to live fully in the light, to be strong, to be healed, to be joyful.

As I am filled with light, I feel the light emerging from me.

In the fullness of the light, I recognize Christ.

"It is the Lord."

+ *Closing:* I enter into deep and heartfelt conversation with Christ, thanking him, glorifying him.

+ *Review of prayer:* In my journal I take note of whatever insights and feelings have surfaced during the time of prayer.

Week 4, Day 4: Like Silver

2 COR. 1:3-7

Blessed be the God and Father of our Lord Jesus Christ, the merciful Father and the God who gives every possible encouragement; he supports us in every hardship, so that we are able to come to the support of others, in every hardship of theirs because of the encouragement that we ourselves receive from God. For just as the sufferings of Christ overflow into our lives; so too does the encouragement we receive through Christ. So if we have hardships to undergo, this will contribute to your encouragement and your salvation; if we receive encouragement, this is to gain for you the encouragement which enables you to bear with perseverance the same sufferings as we do. So our hope for you is secure in the knowledge that you share the encouragement we receive, no less than the sufferings we bear.

Silver—rare, precious, and noble—is one of the elements found in the earth. Brilliantly lustrous, it reflects almost all of the light that shines on it. Of all the metals, silver has the highest thermal and electrical conductivity. Among the noble elements, it is the most chemically active. Although silver occasionally occurs in nature as a free element, most frequently it is held bound with other metals.

To free silver from its ores, that is, to purify the metal, it must be subjected to a process of refinement. The methods used in the process of the reclamation of silver from the compounds in which it is held are radical, making use of sulfuric acid, alkali, fire, and electrolysis.

The process used to refine silver can be likened to the suffering that is part of authentic Christian life.

Declares Yahweh Sabaoth . . .
I shall pass [them] through the fire,
refine them as silver is refined.

               (Zech. 13:8-9)

If we make a conscious choice to throw in our lot with Christ, we cannot be taken by surprise when we experience the heavy weight of a cross, nor can we be reluctant to fully embrace the sweet consolations of life's joys. If we really believe in Christ and seek to pattern our life after his, then suffering and consolation will be intimately juxtaposed. Christ's dying and rising become our own. In the evolutionary journey of humankind, Christ's life continues to unfold in those who say yes.

We simply cannot have Easter without Lent, nor Lent without Easter.

To commit ourselves to such a radical process is to demand from ourselves an enduring commitment. Our daily life with its internal and external conflicts and darkness is the matrix for the process of our reclamation. The fire and acid of our personal pain serve as the radical elements for our purification and ultimate freedom.

Paradoxically, in the very fire of our reclamation lies a poignant experience of God's presence.

"For he will be like a refiner's fire, like fullers' alkali. He will take this seat as refiner and purifier; he will purify the sons [and daughters] of Levi and refine them like gold and silver, so that they can make the offering to Yahweh with uprightness." (Mal. 3:2–3)

We are not alone!

With God's presence comes, also, the strength that enables us to meet the rigors demanded in personal transformation. We are literally comforted into strength; the root word of comfort is *fortis,* which means strength.

"Comfort, comfort my people, says your God" (Isa. 40:1, RSV).

We need only to remember the many love gifts we have received during our life. Among the many are the people who have carried God's love to us, the solutions to problems that outstrip our expectations, seemingly contradictory circumstances that surprisingly yield sterling enlightenment. God's comforts are not saccharine! They are powerful consolations that, in turn, enable us to comfort others as they, too, endure their purification.

The final blessing in this process of refinement is a world community reclaimed and transfigured. It is an Easter world freed from the cross of death.

In God's greatest gift to us, the gift of Christ, God released the power of life.
"'I came to cast fire upon the earth'" (Luke 12:49, RSV).
The Risen Christ is our supreme consolation!

Suggested Approach to Prayer: Silver Vessel

+ *Daily prayer pattern:* (See pages 1 and 2.)
I quiet myself and relax in the presence of God.
I declare my dependency on God.

+ *Grace:* I ask for the gift of a deep share in the creative joy of the Risen Christ.

+ *Method:* Contemplation, as on page 3.
In my imagination, I hold in my left hand a substantial nugget of the purest silver.
I enjoy the feel of it in my hand, the weight of it, the soft smoothness of its surface.
I appreciate its beautiful luster, how it reflects the light as if it contains light.
For a space of time, I simply enjoy the silver.
Then I visualize the silver being molded into a cup or chalice of my own design. I imagine it in great detail, its size, shape, and embellishments.
If the idea of drawing the cup feels natural to me, I do so, as simply or as elaborately as I wish.

+ *Closing:* I enter into conversation with Christ, speaking whatever my heart prompts me to say as I reflect on my experience of prayer.

+ *Review of prayer:* I note in my journal whatever feelings or insights have surfaced during the time of prayer.

Week 4, Day 5: Look at Me

1 COR. 3:16–17

Did you not realise that you are a temple of God with the Spirit of God living in you?

"Oh, mama . . . just look at me one minute as though you really saw me" (111, act 3).

Emily, the protagonist in Thornton Wilder's play *Our Town*, has died and been allowed to return, though unseen, to the world of the living. She was granted one day in her life on which to return, and she chose a happy day, her twelfth birthday. Her experience, however, is not as joyous as she had anticipated it would be.

In the heightened awareness that death has given her, Emily sees with new eyes. What she witnesses causes her to grieve "how in the dark live persons are." They simply do not "look at one another. . . . All that was going on and we never noticed" (act 3).

"Just look at me one minute as though you really saw me."

If we listened within the stillness of our hearts, we would hear these words echo throughout creation. If we bent our ear to the earth—the rocks, the soil, the grass—we would hear the words, "look at me."

If we leaned near, the animals, both wild and tame, would reverberate the plea, "look at me."

If we listened attentively, even the sound of the sea would carry the message, "look at me."

And if we looked, really looked, we would see inscribed in each person's eyes the words, "look at me . . . as though you really saw me."

If we looked, what would we see? No doubt, we would see the cherished depths of the person. We would catch a glimpse of God!

All creation is diaphanous with God's presence. Every fragment of life, no matter how minute, shares in the holiness of the whole. All of creation is gifted by God with God. All is holy. All is worthy of our contemplation.

To see God in our world and in ourselves is to live fully in the embrace of God's gift of love. It is to hold firmly, tenderly the integrity of all of creation.

To be seen and to see with the eyes of love is to further release the energy of love. Energy sparks energy! As it builds momentum, a oneness of being evolves. All of creation becomes an alleluia community of holiness. "Did you not realize that . . . the Spirit of God [was] living in you?"

Emily challenges us, "Do any human beings ever realise life while they live it? —every minute, every minute?" (act 3).

Suggested Approach to Prayer: The Gift of Each Moment

+ *Daily prayer pattern:* (See pages 1 and 2.)
  I quiet myself and relax in the presence of God.
  I declare my dependency on God.

+ *Grace:* I ask for the gift of sharing deeply in the joy of the Risen Christ.

+ *Method:* Contemplation, as on page 3.
  I imagine that I, like Emily, have died. I, too, have been granted one day on which I may return to the living world.

  I consider which day of my life I will return to.

  Remembering the details of the day, the place, the people, I move through the day.

  I ask myself what it is that I most yearn to relive and to live more fully.

  I sensitively touch the many surfaces and textures that come before me as I move through my day. How do I feel now as I look at them with new vision?

  I call myself to be aware of the scents that permeate the spaces of my day, that is, the scent of cooking, of different family members and friends, of nature. I am aware of my own scent.

  Recalling the meals of the day that I chose, I savor the taste of the food, relishing the many distinctive flavors.

  What sounds do I listen for more acutely? Is it the timbre of my father's voice? the sound of my mother's footsteps? the wind? a particular piece of music . . . ?

I thoughtfully ponder, Whose face would I most love to see? What do I see in that person's face as I look deeply?

As I look with sensitivity at my remembered day, I pause frequently to cherish with reverence the gift of each person, each place, each thing that made up the fabric of that day. I allow myself the space and time with which to enjoy fully all that I missed at the initial moment.

+ *Closing:* In prayer, I ask that God would give me the gift of this new vision so that I might perceive the preciousness of each moment, each person, and so that I might perceive how God is present and shows forth in them.

To such a fullness of love given, I desire to respond with the fullness of myself. I pray:

Take, Lord, and receive all my liberty, my memory, my understanding, and my entire will—all that I have and call my own. You have given it all to me. To you, Lord, I return it. Everything is yours; do with it what you will. Give me only your love and your grace. That is enough for me. (43, p. 141)

+ *Review of prayer:* In my journal I take note of feelings and insights that have surfaced during my prayer.

Week 4, Day 6: Repetition

Suggested Approach to Prayer

+ *Daily prayer pattern:* (See pages 1 and 2.)
I quiet myself and relax in the presence of God.
I declare my dependency on God.

+ *Grace:* I ask for a deep sharing in the joy of the Risen Christ.

+ *Method:* Repetition, as on page 6.

In preparation, I review my prayer periods by reading my journal of the past week. I select for my repetition the period of prayer in which I was most deeply moved or one in which I experienced a lack of emotional response or one in which I was grasped with insight or one in which I experienced confusion. I use the method with which I approached the passage initially. I open myself to hear again God's word to me in that particular passage.

+ *Review of prayer:* I write in my journal any feelings, experiences, or insights that have surfaced in this second listening.

Week 5, Day 1: Fountain of Life

MATT. 28:16–20

Meanwhile the eleven disciples set out for Galilee, to the mountain where Jesus had arranged to meet them. When they saw him they fell down before him, though some hesitated. Jesus came up and spoke to them. He said, "All authority in heaven and on earth has been given to me. Go, therefore, make disciples of all nations; baptise them in the name of the Father and of the Son and of the Holy Spirit, and teach them to observe all the commands I gave you. And look, I am with you always; yes, to the end of time."

In every age, the human heart thirsts for signs of love and hope. For some people today, Aquarius, striding on the horizon carrying a pail of refreshing water, becomes a symbol of this profound longing.

When Christ, in the power of the Spirit, emerged from the waters of baptism, he brought to the world the waters of everlasting life (John 4:13–15). His words and actions, preaching, teaching, and healing, carried the life of the Spirit. Through the baptism of his death and resurrection (Luke 12:50), he has entered into the fullness of the power of the Holy Spirit. This is the unlimited power that breaks into and transcends all time and space. With the fullness of the Spirit, Christ authors the power of new life within us. As baptized followers of him, we, too, become energized into the dynamic flow of love that characterizes an evolving relationship with God and with each other.

As sharers of this spirit we are empowered and commissioned to preach, to teach, and to heal as Christ did. Through Christ resurrected, the power of the Holy Spirit released into the world draws all things into God. Through the Spirit's power, a new awareness of integration and possibility arises from the wells of our deepest consciousness. A fresh kind of life is starting!

To welcome this New Age is to envision love as a continually flowing fountain. From the mouth of this fountain issues forth the sustaining word of God for all peoples. Springing from its divine, cosmic center, the genesis waters of creation are ever flowing into the womb of Christ's birthing, ever spilling over into the baptismal font of the creative spirit of the resurrection. This tripartite fountain of life forms a complete circle that continually cleanses, purifies, refreshes, and regenerates.

Even in the figure of Aquarius we are reminded of the Easter task of each person to be water bearers for others. Christians baptized with and into the consciousness of Christ have the power and the vision to bring the life-giving water of the Omega into the desert dryness of our present world.

Suggested Approach to Prayer: The Water Bearer

+ *Daily prayer pattern:* (See pages 1 and 2.)
  I quiet myself and relax in the presence of God.
  I declare my dependency on God.

+ *Grace:* I ask for the gift of sharing deeply in the joy of the Risen Christ.

+ *Method:* Contemplation, as on page 3.
  I form an image of myself with the disciples on the mountain. I see in great detail the day and the journey. I note the excitement on the faces of the disciples, their eagerness to see Christ. I am aware of my own feelings of anticipation.

I see Jesus approach us. I watch as the disciples fall down before him in worship.

I listen to the words of Jesus as he speaks to us. I hear him declare his full authority and power. I especially focus on his words commissioning us to make disciples of all nations, to baptize, and to teach.

I form an image of the world to which we are being sent. I see its vast areas of desert dryness. I see the people who thirst, clamoring for the waters of life. I see their desperate struggle and search for a source of water. I am aware of how many have succumbed to desperation, unaware of the meaning of their inner thirst.

I go to Christ as to a well and drink deeply of his Spirit. I allow my own spirit to experience the renewal and refreshment of this living water.

I consider to whom I will bring the water of life, his presence. I consider how I will carry it, how my actions and words will convey this life.

As I gaze at the vast need, the thirst of the people of the world, I hear the words of Christ saying to me, "I am with you always; yes, to the end of time."

I consider how I am not alone, that my life as water bearer is in partnership with Christ and sustained in his Spirit.

+ *Closing:* I confide my life to Christ, thanking him for the joy of being called to co-labor with him. I pray the Our Father.

+ *Review of prayer:* I note in my journal the insights and feelings that have surfaced during my prayer.

Week 5, Day 2: Woman of Wisdom

ISA. 43:8–13

Bring forward the people that is blind, yet has eyes,
that is deaf and yet has ears.
Let all the nations assemble,
let the peoples gather here!
Which of them has proclaimed this
and revealed things to us in the past?
Let them bring their witnesses to justify themselves,
let others hear and say, "It is true."
You yourselves are my witnesses, declares Yahweh,
and the servant whom I have chosen,
so that you may know and believe me
and understand that it is I.
No god was formed before me,
nor will be after me.
I, I am Yahweh,
there is no other Saviour but me.
I have revealed, have saved, and have proclaimed,
not some foreigner among you.
You are my witnesses, declares Yahweh,

I am God, yes, from eternity I am.
No one can deliver from my hand;
when I act, who can thwart me?

Hakmot*, God's servant and witness, has come to the gates of the city to proclaim Yahweh's saving acts. Her face is etched with the pain and promise of her life, the history of Israel. Her body carries the burden of many years, yet glows

*Hebrew feminine form of wisdom

with the strength of ever-renewing youth. She is known by her people as חָכְמָה ,
woman of wisdom.

Hakmot speaks:
I was there in Egypt
    carrying, to the rhythm of the whip,
        bricks of sorrow
      pressed down with fear
      crushed in heart
    without home, voice, or son.

I stood on the shores of the Reed Sea
    at my back terror galloped
    before me rose threatening waves.

Forty years I thirsted
    my flesh lashed by sand and sun
    desperately birthing calves of gold
    burning wind whirling an agony of betrayal.

God was with us
    bush blazing
        unconsumable hope
    liberating path
        seaway to freedom
    rock springing water
        morning dew of blossoming manna.

Hakmot speaks:
I was there in Jerusalem
    seeing through tears of unbelief
        loss and grief bundled tightly
        spilled blood of infant life
    burdened for a thousand miles.

I wept in Babylon
       Gershom, Gershom
       lonely, a stranger
       bereft
       without country, without king, without altar
       seventy years my people cried;
       seventy years my heart bled home.

God was with us
       consoling presence
              promise of strength
       spirit of the temple
              dweller within the word
       Chebar's fullest dream
              living home.

Hakmot, woman of wisdom, continues through time to nourish at her breast true witnesses of God. She teaches her disciples to recognize God's presence in history; she inspires them to give witness to Emmanuel, God-with-us.

Hakmot, wisdom, stands in the Easter dawn proclaiming to all the nations, "Listen, you deaf! Look and see, you blind!" (Isa. 42:18).

"Yahweh our God is the one, the only Yahweh. You must love Yahweh your God with all your heart, with all your soul, with all your strength." (Deut. 6:4–5)

Suggested Approach to Prayer: Tell the Children

+ *Daily prayer pattern:* (See pages 1 and 2.)
    I quiet myself and relax in the presence of God.
    I declare my dependency on God.

+ *Grace:* I ask for the gift of sharing deeply the joy of the Risen Christ.

+ *Method:* Contemplation, as on page 3.

I visualize myself as a storyteller. I see myself seated, surrounded by children who snuggle close to me. Some cling to my arm. Others are on my lap, while I embrace still others. They listen with great attention as I tell them of the history of my life and of our family.

I re-create for them the events and the people that have shaped the particular charism of our family.

In great detail, I relate to them the memories of the pain and struggles we endured.

I share with them the joy and times of celebration.

In the telling of the story, I sensitively impart to the children the spirit that animated our experience, that is, courage, fear, determination, perseverance, happiness, surprise.

I share with them the ways in which our God has sustained us through our sufferings to bring us to greater knowledge and understanding, to love.

I write the story in my journal if doing so seems natural to me.

+ *Closing:* Filled with gratitude for so great a love, I let my heart speak intimately to my God. I pray the Our Father.

+ *Review of prayer:* I note in my journal the insights and feelings that have surfaced during the time of prayer.

Week 5, Day 3: Encountering Joy

1 COR. 15:3–8

The tradition I handed on to you in the first place, a tradition which I had myself received, was that Christ died for our sins, in accordance with the scriptures, and that he was buried; and that on the third day, he was raised to life, in accordance with the scriptures; and that he appeared to Cephas; and later to the Twelve; and next he appeared to more than five hundred of the brothers at the same time, most of whom are still with us, though some have fallen asleep; then he appeared to James, and then to all the apostles. Last of all he appeared to me too, as though I was a child born abnormally.

"'Look, I bring you news of great joy, a joy to be shared by the whole people'" (Luke 2:10).

Christ, resurrected, appeared to Peter and the Twelve, to the five hundred, to James, and to Paul. "The glory of the Lord shone round them" (Luke 2:9).

He whom they loved had died. He whom they had followed had been buried, sealed in the tomb. He whose death had aborted their hope made himself seen.

"The glory of the Lord shone round them."

What is invisible is made visible!

The joy of their encounter with the Risen Christ balanced the loss and separation they experienced at his death. It was in this meeting that the disciples experienced a oneness within themselves.

Encountering Christ, risen, they discovered their deepest identity. This grace of oneness grounding their identity in Christ enabled them to see the unseen. In this new strength their heart was laid open to fully receive Christ and to emerge in him. In the experience of oneness in themselves, they came to unity with each other.

Trusting in the experience that resonated within them, the disciples knew that the encounters they had with Christ after his death occurred always at his initiative. The events of his death and burial had given them an experience of their own powerlessness. Each disciple carried within himself the knowledge and burden of his own weakness. Peter suffered the nearly overwhelming guilt of his threefold denial of Christ; Paul was never able to forget that he had persecuted Christ in the Christian community.

They were acutely aware that each Easter moment was the pure gift of the fullness of Christ's love for them.

It was in their heart emptied of pride that Christ entered and let himself be seen. Joy found a home.

As a large centrifugal force from within, joy spiraled the disciples outward from Jerusalem.

In the moment of the disciples' encounter with Christ, the dream of the twelve tribes of ancient Israel came true. Through the "glad tidings" of the mission of the twelve apostles, the prophesied community of love was birthed.

Suggested Approach to Prayer: Easter Gift

+ *Daily prayer pattern:* (See pages 1 and 2.)
   I quiet myself and relax in the presence of God.
   I declare my dependency on God.

+ *Grace:* I ask for the gift of sharing deeply in the joy of the Risen Christ.

+ *Method:* Mantra, as on page 4.
   I consider the area of my powerlessness, my particular vulnerability, and the corresponding gift I need from Christ, for example: my doubt, his confidence; my denial, his faithfulness; my pride, his humility; my fear, his courage, and so on.

   Trusting in Christ's forgiving love, I open my heart to receive and to see his resurrected presence.

   I pray in mantra fashion, "Lord Jesus Christ, Risen Son, grant me the gift of your spirit of _____ [the gift that meets my need]."

+ *Closing:* I enter into conversation with Christ, thanking him for his Easter presence in my life. I pray the Our Father.

+ *Review of prayer:* I note in my journal the insights and feelings that have surfaced during my prayer.

Week 5, Day 4: O Admirable Exchange

ACTS 1:6–11

Now having met together, they asked him, "Lord, has the time come for you to restore the kingdom of Israel?" He replied, "It is not for you to know times or dates that the Father has decided by his own authority, but you will receive the power of the Holy Spirit which will come on you, and then you will be my witnesses not only in Jerusalem but throughout Judaea and Samaria, and indeed to earth's remotest end."

As he said this he was lifted up while they looked on, and a cloud took him from their sight. They were still staring into the sky as he went when suddenly two men in white were standing beside them and they said, "Why are you Galileans standing here looking into the sky? This Jesus who has been taken up from you into heaven will come back in the same way as you have seen him go to heaven."

Christ's ascension is the announcement that heaven has begun!

The end times are upon us! The raising of Jesus is the raising of the world into the holiness of God's presence. Hereafter no one or no event can alter that. In Christ a part of us and our world has been taken into blessedness. Our world has been definitively received into God's heart.

O admirable exchange!

The circle is complete! At the birth of Christ, God came into our humanness; in his ascension, Christ drew our humanness into God. From the beginning God has walked with all of creation (Gen. 3:8). From the beginning we have been drawn into the blessedness of God's life (Gen. 17:1). At Christmas we celebrate God's continual birthing within us and within our world; in the Easter ascension mystery, we celebrate our life and our world's continually being raised in the Creator.

Alleluia! Our life, our world are held in the joyful momentum of the spiraling circle of life!

To believe this is to change one's entire perspective on the world. It is to live in the confidence and courage that nothing can separate us from the love of Christ (Rom. 8:39). Everything is penetrated by this love.

There will be sin, pain, and violence. There will be fear and trembling. Even these are not outside the circle of God's love. The suffering and surrender of the cross is part of the dynamic of Christ's continuing victory. Standing firm in the conviction that Christ is present in everything, we will not be overwhelmed. We will walk in trust, poised and confident that nothing is greater than the love that surrounds and supports us.

We will know, deep in our heart that "everything that happens in the world now is either an effect of his victory or a last-ditch battle of those worldly powers that were conquered by his cross" (90, no. 246).

Suggested Approach to Prayer: Exchange of Hearts

+ *Daily prayer pattern:* (See pages 1 and 2.)
  I quiet myself and relax in the presence of God.
  I declare my dependency on God.

+ *Grace:* I ask for the gift of a deep sharing in the joy of the Risen Christ.

+ *Method:* Meditation, as on page 3.
  Saint Catherine of Siena is said to have celebrated the Feast of the Ascension by asking Jesus to take her heart and to give his to her. Interiorly she offered her whole self to Christ. The story is told that immediately following her offering of self, she experienced an acute inner emptiness and sense of loss. Some time later her prayer came to fruitfulness when she experienced being filled with an overwhelming sense of God's love and joy.

This spontaneous prayer on the part of Catherine speaks to us of the inner meaning of the Feast of the Ascension. Christ enters within our humanity and assumes our humanness into himself; a true exchange of hearts.

From a life of faithful prayer grounded in the trust, confidence, and strength of God's love, Saint Catherine's powerful influence reached far beyond herself to shape the world of her time. She persuaded the pope to return to Rome from Avignon, and she mediated feuds between rival city-states.

Catherine's love of God inspires our prayer and leads us courageously beyond ourselves. Her example of contemplation in action serves as a model for our own assumption of responsibility in the modern world as it moves toward completion in Christ.

Following the lead of this holy woman, I prayerfully offer my heart, my entire being, to Christ.

I beg Christ to penetrate my whole self with his presence, the heart of love. I ask God to raise my entire being and the whole world, all of creation, into blessedness.

+ *Closing:* I close with a heartfelt conversation with Christ, with deep thankfulness and praise. I pray the Our Father.

+ *Review of prayer:* I note in my journal the insights and feelings that surfaced in my prayer. If so moved, I write my offering.

Week 5, Day 5: Easter Now

REV. 21:1–7

Then I saw a new heaven and a new earth; the first heaven and the first earth had disappeared now, and there was no longer any sea. I saw the holy city, the new Jerusalem, coming down out of heaven from God, as prepared as a bride dressed for her husband. Then I heard a loud voice call from the throne, "Look, here God lives among human beings. He will make his home among them; they will be his people, and he will be their God, God-with-them. He will wipe away all tears from their eyes; there will be no more death, and no more mourning or sadness or pain. The world of the past is gone."

Then the One sitting on the throne spoke. "Look, I am making the whole of creation new. Write this, 'What I am saying is trustworthy and will come true.'" Then he said to me, "It has already happened. I am the Alpha and the Omega, the Beginning and the End. I will give water from the well of life free to anybody who is thirsty; anyone who proves victorious will inherit these things; and I will be his God and he will be my son."

"The roses were white but with a gentle blush of pink . . . the bridesmaid's dress was lavender, the color then in fashion. . . . My dress cost nineteen dollars, more than an entire week's wage!"

A seventy-seven-year-old woman shared the story of her wedding with her daughter. As she spoke, her eyes brightened and her face glowed, reflecting the youthfulness that was hers on her wedding day.

Her daughter was delighted by how present her mother was in this moment of sharing and awed at how alive the wedding day remained in her mother's heart.

Love, which had endured the separation from her husband through his death forty years earlier, leapt the distance between life and death. In this precious moment, heaven and earth were joined. In the heart of the elderly widow lives the bride of her youth. She waits in the union of the "not-quite-yet," anticipating the joy when she will fully embrace and be embraced.

The radical human longing to love and to be loved is the energy that has reverberated throughout all of history. It is the bridal song of hope that resounds through all of life, stretching creation toward the final transformation of the world, to paradise regained, to the new Jerusalem. It is the joy of Easter's celebration.

Hope is visible as the Easter candle plunges into the baptismal womb (80, Easter Vigil) of the earth waters. A new birth of love surfaces out of the chaotic waters, long feared as the abode of monsters. Penetrated with Christ's Spirit, the waters are empowered to quench forever the thirst of creation's longing.

Christ has died; Christ has risen; his Spirit is with us.

To place ourselves fully present to this Easter mystery is to live in the love energy of Christ's resurrection. To believe, to be present to Christ, risen, is to liberate into the world the deepest reality of love's potential. To live in the *now* of Easter is to shake off the daze of mystic trance and lay claim to love's freedom.

To share in love's release is to rise with Christ. It is to live the Christ-life, bringing healing through woundedness, infusing meaning into the banal monotony of everyday life.

The Alpha word of Easter is to live the Omega word of love. This love conquers all death, all darkness, every tear (Song of Songs 8:6). Easter love knows no bounds; it is totally receptive, faithful, and unconditional. The one unifying force of the universe, reconciling all of creation and drawing all into union, is love.

> love is a place
> & through this place of
> love move
> (with brightness of peace)
> all places
>
> yes is a world
> & in this world of
> yes live
> (skilfully curled)
> all worlds
>   (34, no. 58)

Christ's love confirms the fulfillment of God's everlasting vow to us—God's beloved. The bridal yes seals forever a covenant of joy.

Suggested Approach to Prayer: Bridal Mantra

+ *Daily prayer pattern:* (See pages 1 and 2.)
I quiet myself and relax in the presence of God.
I declare my dependency on God.

+ *Grace:* I ask for the gift of sharing in the joy of the Risen Christ.

+ *Method:* Mantra, as on page 4.
I envision myself before the Risen Christ. I see myself as a bride, arrayed in the light of Christ. (Men do this too!)
I relax totally in the joy of Christ's penetrating love.
I receive into my being his vow of everlasting love. I hear Christ pledge his unconditional acceptance of me.
Before such love, I respond by prayerfully reciting, aloud if possible, the Prayer of Love and Praise found on page 12.
I repeat this prayer in mantra fashion, savoring any particular word or phrase that touches me most deeply.

+ *Closing:* I simply enjoy the presence of love, returning love for love. I pray the Our Father.

+ *Review of prayer:* I note in my journal the words of the prayer that have particularly touched me, as well as any insights or feelings that have surfaced.

Week 5, Day 6: Repetition

Suggested Approach to Prayer

+ *Daily prayer pattern:* (See pages 1 and 2.)
I quiet myself and relax in the presence of God.
I declare my dependency on God.

+ *Grace:* I ask for a deep sharing in the joy of the Risen Christ.

+ *Method:* Repetition, as on page 6.
In preparation, I review my prayer periods by reading my journal of the past week. I select for my repetition the period of prayer in which I was most deeply moved or one in which I experienced a lack of emotional response or one in which I was grasped with insight or one in which I experienced confusion. I use the method with which I approached the passage initially. I open myself to hear again God's word to me in that particular passage.

+ *Review of prayer:* I write in my journal any feelings, experiences, or insights that have surfaced in this second listening.

Week 6, Day 1: Easter Child

JOHN 3:16

"For this is how God loved the world:
he gave his only Son."

Easter is a little child!

Nothing could speak more appropriately of Christ's resurrection than the image of a child; nothing could speak more radically of the ongoing birthing, gifting, and laboring of God in the world.

From southwestern artist Ted De Grazia's palette has emerged an image of a young child standing erect with arms fully extended. An aura of bright light radiates from the child and a globe crown rests upon his small head. The child is enthroned on an altar banked with lighted candles in the center of a tomb-like sanctuary. The entire scene is encircled with flowers of many colors. The tomb is attended by a youthful feminine angel.

De Grazia's artistic rendering of the resurrection is fresh, delightful, and prophetic.

Through the eyes of this artist our vision is charmed, then enticed into an expanded awareness of the presence and meaning of the Risen Christ in our life.

Through the use of a child as a resurrection symbol, De Grazia completes for us the regenerative, healing, and empowering cycle of Christ's life, the circle of God's love. We are led to return again to the manger. We see the Infant Jesus, God's only son, nestled in the straw of the cave. We hear the angels sing the joy of God's presence among us.*

The reflection on De Grazia's Easter child reminds us of another child, another son. We see Isaac, his young back burdened with firewood as he labors up the mountain. Our hearts are filled with knowing tears of how anguished his father, Abraham, felt at the thought of losing his only son (Gen. 22:1–18).

---

*Drawing on the spirituality of the Arizona Yaqui people, De Grazia's art compels us into a dramatic shift of consciousness. Its primitive yet profound grasp of the significance of the Christ event offers to Western spirituality an intuitive right-brained orientation and balance that it so desperately needs.

Then again, we think of another son. We stand at the foot of the cross. Our entire beings are stretched to imagine what it must have been for God to hand over his only son. Perhaps it is only in imagining the tears of God that we can possibly begin to fathom the depth of God's love for our world.

The cave of the birth and the tomb of the new Easter life form the definitive circle of love. The love energy of this continuing labor of God's work of love is the vivifying principle of the universe. Each particle of creation, however infinitesimal, is rife with this life energy.

All of creation is encircled by the helical energy of God's love at work in the world. From within, everything is ordered and moves, spiraling forward this labor of God. The dance of opposites—solar and lunar, feminine and masculine—is delicately reconciled in the yin and yang rhythm of creation. There is no beginning or end, no space or limitation to this ongoing work of God. God labors lovingly, circling and circling, bringing forth the new life of Easter.

God's love, like God, "is a circle whose center is everywhere and whose circumference is nowhere!" (29, p. 36).

Suggested Approach to Prayer: God at Work

+ *Daily prayer pattern:* (See pages 1 and 2.)
    I quiet myself and relax in the presence of God.
    I declare my dependency on God.

+ *Grace:* I ask for the gift of sharing deeply in the joy of the Risen Christ.

+ *Method:* Meditation, as on page 3.
    I consider how God works and labors for me.

I reflect on how God behaves like one who labors in all things created. I consider the heavens, the earth, the plants, and the animals, how God gives them being, preserves them, and gives them growth and sensation.

I reflect on how God labors for me, within me. I recall concrete situations in my life when God, like a mother or father, entered into my struggles for life. I consider how the Creator has labored in me like a potter with clay, like a mother giving birth, like a mighty energy blowing life into dead bones (43, p. 141).

I consider how God labors to share his life and love with me.

I consider how, in Christ, the love God has for me led Christ to be born into the world and brought him to death on a cross in order to bring forth the newness of the resurrection.

Before such love, I desire to respond with the fullness of myself. I pray:

Take, Lord, and receive all my liberty, my memory, my understanding, and my entire will—all that I have and call my own. You have given it all to me. To you, Lord, I return it. Everything is yours; do with it what you will. Give me only your love and your grace. That is enough for me. (43, p. 141)

+ *Review of prayer:* In my journal I take note of feelings and insights that have surfaced during my prayer.

Week 6, Day 2: In Fire and Wind

ACTS 2:1–11

When Pentecost day came round, they had all met together when suddenly there came from heaven a sound as of a violent wind which filled the entire house in which they were sitting; and there appeared to them tongues as of fire; these separated and came to rest on the head of each of them. They were all filled with the Holy Spirit and began to speak different languages as the Spirit gave them power to express themselves.

Now there were devout men living in Jerusalem from every nation under heaven, and at this sound they all assembled, and each one was bewildered to hear these men speaking his own language. They were amazed and astonished. "Surely," they said, "all these men speaking are Galileans? How does it happen that each of us hears them in his own native language? Parthians, Medes and Elamites; people from Mesopotamia, Judaea and Cappadocia, Pontus and Asia, Phrygia and Pamphylia, Egypt and the parts of Libya round Cyrene; residents of Rome—Jews and proselytes alike—Cretans and Arabs; we hear them preaching in our own language about the marvels of God."

Peals of thunder

    Lightning flashes

        Trumpet blasts

Violent and powerful wind

      Mountains wrapped in smoke

    Devouring fire

    Tongues of fire

Earth trembles! God comes!

Earth itself announces God's coming (Exod. 19:16,18; 24:17; Acts 2:2). Wind and fire serve as heralds of God's presence, breaking through all barriers.

Stirred by God's presence, we find an affinity with the freedom of the wind and the ecstasy of fire. Only primitive earth symbols are powerful enough to lay hold on and express, in some measure, the profound and elusive inner reality of God's coming. These archetypal symbols resonate into the bowels of our human experience, linking us in solidarity with the deepest reality that dwells within every human spirit. Encountered with the regenerative energy of such symbols, our oneness with all who have come before us provides a clearer understanding of the present and fuels the evolutional progress of all humankind.

The wind and the fire of the upper room set free the mind and heart of the disciples. In the miraculous energy of the Spirit's coming they are, at once, united with those who on Mount Sinai experienced Yahweh as he came "in the form of fire" (Exod. 19:18), and they are missioned into the future to bring the fire of Christ's Spirit to the whole earth (Luke 12:49).

Fences of division and walls of fear and doubt crumble as Christ's Spirit quickens each heart and enlivens each tongue. Unrestrainable joy is released! Every caution and competition immediately is superceded by an infusion of wisdom that recognizes and honors Christ's Spirit uniquely expressed in the gift-edness of each individual. The division and confusion of Babel is reversed and replaced with a clarity of understanding and appreciation of other nations and peoples (Gen. 11:1–9). Distinctions no longer exist between Jew and Gentile, male and female, master and slave. All share and are united in the same Spirit (Gal. 3:28).

Fire has come!
                        illuminating
        regenerative   renewing
                purifying
                        transforming
                    fusion!
                    freedom!
Spirit of Christ, come!

Suggested Approach to Prayer: In the Upper Room

+ *Daily prayer pattern:* (See pages 1 and 2.)
I quiet myself and relax in the presence of God.
I declare my dependency on God.

+ *Grace:* I ask for the gift of sharing deeply and fully in the joy of the Spirit of the Risen Christ.

+ *Method:* Contemplation, as on page 3.
Considering that it is the Spirit that relives in us all the events of Christ's earthly life, and "makes us present to his mysteries" (37, p. 248), I place myself in the upper room with the disciples of Christ.

Forming an image of the room in great detail, I consider the kind of day it is, my immediate surroundings, and so on.

I note who is present in the room, their facial expressions, their conversations. I note particularly the feeling tone of the room and become aware of my own feelings and anticipation.

I imagine a sound like a powerful wind filling the room. I am aware of people's responses to this sound. I note any feelings that surface within me as the sound reverberates around me.

I envision what appear to be tongues of fire separating and coming to rest on the head of each person.

Resting in the experience of this coming of the Spirit, I allow the presence to fill my being.

I am aware of the feelings and insights that surface within me.

I see and share in the disciples' joy and energy of the Spirit.

+ *Closing:* I ask that Christ's Spirit would illuminate me with wisdom, renew me in energy and hope, unite me in love, and release me in freedom. I beg that my life, all my decisions and plans, would be under the firm direction of Christ's Spirit. I give thanks for the fire of the Spirit coming to me, into our world. I pray the Our Father.

+ *Review of prayer:* I note in my journal whatever feelings and insights have surfaced during my prayer.

Week 6, Day 3: The Golden Thread

GAL. 5:1,25

Christ set us free, so that we should remain free. Stand firm, then, and do not let yourselves be fastened again to the yoke of slavery.

Since we are living by the Spirit, let our behaviour be guided by the Spirit.

"To be or not to be?" At the heart of Hamlet's probing monologue lies the quest for freedom.

If we were to express in one word the hunger of the human heart, the word would be *freedom*. If we were to express in one word the hope of the human heart, the word would be *freedom*.

Freedom is the very essence of the human spirit, "an exceptional sign of the divine image within." Freedom is the spirit from which all authenticity and joy radiate outward. "Only in freedom can [humankind] direct [itself] toward goodness" (1, "The Church Today," no. 17). It is the ultimate stance of truth and love before God and the world (John 8:32).

If we are to live in the full dignity of freedom, it follows that our decisions will "not result from blind internal impulse nor from mere external pressure" (1, "The Church Today," no. 17). Rather, we will make every effort to seek counsel from the Spirit dwelling within ourselves. All of our life choices and decisions will be based on and arise from an acute awareness of our dependency on God's love. The powerful energy of the Spirit is like a golden thread that gently keeps us in touch with and open to receiving the wisdom and courage of Christ. To be free is to live in the Spirit.

To live in the freedom of Christ is to be delivered from slavery. Ironically, however, it is possible to be a slave yet be free. To be externally enslaved does not necessarily imply or dictate internal bondage, nor does external freedom assure interior freedom. The factor determining freedom or slavery is our response to the conviction that God is active within the events and happenings in our life. The depth of this personal faith response receives its impetus from the energy of the indwelling Spirit.

To live our life alienated from the Spirit within is to be enslaved. Some enslavements are easily recognized. A person with a ball and chain attached to his or her ankle is obviously not free. It is also easy to see the enslavement of an addict.

Enslavement is rampant and takes on many guises. "Good works" themselves, apart from the Spirit, can become as enslaving as a ball and chain. The subtlety and hiddenness that sometimes characterize slavery are not to be underestimated. Any activity or attitude that springs from a disordered, uncentered motive subjects us to the dangers of the enslavement that Christ calls us to reject.

Excessive attachment to a good is extremely seductive and potentially life-threatening. Frequently a thin line lies between what is authentically of the Spirit and what is self-serving and ultimately destructive. We all know people with good intentions who nevertheless have driven themselves and others to illness and death. Someplace along the way, in the original good they set out to do, they were snagged by greed, lust, ambition, or insecurity. It is a sad commentary on the Western world to realize that some prisoners in the horrors of Auschwitz knew a deeper freedom than some of the well-heeled executives of our Wall Street society who are addicted to wealth and power.

Every sector of our society is pervaded with the danger and lure of false freedom. It is a frightening time in which to live. Who, then, can be free?

Paul offers reassurance, "Be guided by the Spirit, and you will no longer yield to self-indulgence" (Gal. 5:16).

To choose to surrender ourselves to the gentle lead of the golden thread of the Spirit is to be released into freedom.

Suggested Approach to Prayer: Discernment

+ *Daily prayer pattern:* (See pages 1 and 2.)
   I quiet myself and relax in the presence of God.
   I declare my dependency on God.

+ *Grace:* I ask for the gift of sharing in the joy and freedom of the Spirit of the Risen Christ.

+ *Method:* If a significant decision is pending, I prayerfully follow through the process of discernment found in appendix 1.

If I'm not involved in a significant decision now, I recall one from the past. With the desire of awakening within myself a deeper awareness of the freedom that is the fruit of decision-making in the Spirit, I subject the previous decision to the process contained in the discernment exercise found in appendix 1.

Week 6, Day 4: Festival of Joy

JOHN 7:37; 8:12

On the last day, the great day of the festival, Jesus stood and cried out:
"Let anyone who is thirsty come to me!"
I am the light of the world.

𝔜𝔬𝔲 𝔞𝔯𝔢 𝔠𝔬𝔯𝔡𝔦𝔞𝔩𝔩𝔶 𝔦𝔫𝔳𝔦𝔱𝔢𝔡 𝔱𝔬
𝔞 𝔖𝔲𝔨𝔨𝔬𝔱𝔥 𝔠𝔢𝔩𝔢𝔟𝔯𝔞𝔱𝔦𝔬𝔫 𝔬𝔣 𝔩𝔦𝔣𝔢—
𝔞 𝔣𝔢𝔰𝔱𝔦𝔳𝔞𝔩 𝔬𝔣 𝔧𝔬𝔶
𝔴𝔥𝔢𝔫 𝔊𝔬𝔡 𝔒𝔲𝔯 𝔠𝔯𝔢𝔞𝔱𝔬𝔯
𝔴𝔦𝔩𝔩 𝔟𝔢 𝔥𝔬𝔫𝔬𝔯𝔢𝔡 𝔞𝔫𝔡 𝔭𝔯𝔞𝔦𝔰𝔢𝔡.

This invitation is being extended to all people. The occasion of this celebration is, like the ancient Jewish harvest festival of Sukkoth, a time to joyously express gratitude and awe for God's gracious and abundant goodness.

The ancient Feast of Sukkoth included various rituals that offer a fullness of symbolic meanings for our understanding of God's love. Two of the more beautiful rites were the libation, when water was lavishly poured over the sacrificial altar, and the illumination, when the temple courtyard was lighted brightly for the nightlong dancing.

In the observance of the ongoing celebration to which we are invited, the grandeur of God's love will be cherished and remembered. Like water that quenches all thirst, like light that illumines the darkness, God's love is totally present. God's love *is* God. I am the living water; "I am the light."

The invitation to a glad celebration of the heart of our God sings within us. God's love is the song. It is a song of unrestrained love, a song of a love that pours itself freely over all of creation. It sings of a love that shines forth with infinite radiance, warming and enlightening the shadows of our nights.

As God's love spills over, we are created; God's goodness is the wellspring of all created goodness. The justice, compassion, mercy, or beauty that we discover within ourselves and each other has its infinite source in God. Just as a drop of water is a part of the waterfall, just as a beam of light is a part of the sun, so God has entered within us. In each fragment of creation, we discover the wonder of God's wholeness inviting us to joy.

Our most appropriate "repondez s'il vous plaît" to this invitation is to make a gift offering. Only a surrendering, all-inclusive *suscipe*, "offering,"—"Take, Lord, and receive. . . ."—will satisfy the desire of our human heart to enter into a communion with God. The very best we have to offer—our liberty, memory, understanding, and will—has been given to us by God, the one to whom we offer them. What better assurance of acceptance can we have!

There is a continuing generation of joy in the exchange of love between Creator and creature. To enter into this activity of joy is absolute certainty of our own homecoming.

To say yes to joy is to live within the household of God (Eph. 2:19), to be family with the God who mothers and fathers forth all of life. It is to be brother or sister with Christ, to have a share in his laboring to bring all of creation into oneness. To say yes is to enter with Christ, risen, into the living, active energy of the procession of the Holy Spirit, moving forward God's ongoing creation toward the Christ Omega.

The invitation has already been sent.

Time: now
Place: your life.

Are you coming to the festival?

Suggested Approach to Prayer: Suscipe Mantra

+ *Daily prayer pattern:* (See pages 1 and 2.)
  I quiet myself and relax in the presence of God.
  I declare my dependency on God.

+ *Grace:* I ask to share deeply in the joy of the Risen Christ.

+ *Method:* Mantra, as on page 4.
  I reflect on the interior gifts I have received from God, our Creator. I consider that whatever gifts I have within, such as goodness, compassion, power, or

beauty, are from God and represent a share in God's own goodness, compassion, power, and beauty.

Entering into a mantralike prayer, I quiet myself, resting deeply within God's love for me.

Using the beautiful suscipe of Saint Ignatius, I pray.

In an attitude of total surrender, I pray, with every exhalation of breath, "Take, Lord, and receive all my liberty, my memory, my understanding, my entire will."

In an attitude of total receptivity, I pray, with every inhalation of breath, "Your love and your grace are enough for me."

I continue to rest quietly, allowing God's love to wash over me and absorbing the warmth and brightness of God's presence.

Periodically, as I am moved by the Spirit, I repeat the mantra words of the suscipe.

+ *Closing:* I pray:

Take, Lord, and receive all my liberty, my memory, my understanding and my entire will—all that I have and call my own. You have given it all to me. To you, Lord, I return it. Everything is yours; do with it what you will. Give me only your love and your grace. That is enough for me. (43, p. 141)

+ *Review of prayer:* In my journal I take note of feelings and insights that have surfaced during my prayer.

Week 6, Day 5: Repetition

Suggested Approach to Prayer

+ *Daily prayer pattern:* (See pages 1 and 2.)
  I quiet myself and relax in the presence of God.
  I declare my dependency on God.

+ *Grace:* I ask for a deep sharing in the joy of the Risen Christ.

+ *Method:* Repetition, as on page 6.
  In preparation, I review my prayer periods by reading my journal of the past week. I select for my repetition the period of prayer in which I was most deeply moved or one in which I experienced a lack of emotional response or one in which I was grasped with insight or one in which I experienced confusion. I use the method with which I approached the passage initially. I open myself to hear again God's word to me in that particular passage.

+ *Review of prayer:* I write in my journal any feelings, experiences, or insights that have surfaced in this second listening.

Week 6, Day 6: Prayer of the People

EPH. 1:17–23

May the God of our Lord Jesus Christ, the Father of glory, give you a spirit of wisdom and perception of what is revealed, to bring you to full knowledge of him. May he enlighten the eyes of your mind so that you can see what hope his call holds for you, how rich is the glory of the heritage he offers among his holy people, and how extraordinarily great is the power that he has exercised for us believers; this accords with the strength of his power at work in Christ, the power which he exercised in raising him from the dead and enthroning him at his right hand, in heaven, far above every principality, ruling force, power or sovereignty, or any other name that can be named, not only in this age but also in the age to come. He has put all things under his feet, and made him, as he is above all things, the head of the Church; which is his Body, the fullness of him who is filled, all in all.

God, our Creator, as a people hewing a pathway into the twenty-first century, our heart cries out to you.

We cry out in gratitude: Great God of our life, we are filled with awe and thanksgiving before the wonders of our earth, with all its myriad forms of nurturing life. Standing before the splendor displayed in the cosmic movements of the stars and moons and planets, we are humbled by the greatness of your creative presence, and we give you praise.

Almighty God, we deeply thank you for your great love, which brought us each to birth and which continues birthing new life within us.

We cry out in our need: Do not forget us, O God. We are a desperate people, pressed down with the effect of our own irresponsible and destructive behaviors.

Faced with breakdown and collapse on every side, we are overwhelmed with a numbing paralysis of helplessness, fear, and indecision.

Save us, O God!

Have mercy on our children and on our children's children.

Enlighten our heart. Direct us firmly, Creator God, and unrelentingly, to place ourselves and our entire world in your reconciling embrace.

May the urgency of our needs be met with the imperative of your wisdom!

Do not give up on us!

We cry out in hope: In you alone, loving God, we place our trust.

Yours is the power. Free us, Creator, to live in the hope held out for us in your promise to Abraham and Sarah and fulfilled in Jesus your Son. Allow our dry and thirsty spirits to be refreshed and made fertile by the wellspring of this hope.

Yours is the glory. Fill us, O God, with a joy of the resurrection and the peace of Christ's risen Spirit.

Celebrate with new and enduring energy your life within us.

Recall to our heart that we are not alone; we are bonded in love with all the saints, those who have gone before us and those who today believe in you and are committed to work toward a new age, the Christ Omega.

Our hearts cry out:

All glory to you, God, our Creator;

All glory to you, Christ, our power and our peace;

All glory to you, Holy Spirit, our joy and our freedom.

Amen. Alleluia!

Suggested Approach to Prayer: Prayer of Recollection

+ *Daily prayer pattern:* (See pages 1 and 2.)
  I quiet myself and relax in the presence of God.
  I declare my dependency on God.

+ *Grace:* I ask to share deeply in the joy of the Risen Christ.

+ *Method:* Using the prayer of the people above, I recollect my life experiences.

As in a meditative reading, I ponder each phrase. Interiorly I expand it and offer it to God with my own gratitude, my own needs, and my own hopes.

+ *Closing:* I open my heart to speak simply, lovingly, intimately to Jesus risen and present. I close with an Our Father.

+ *Review of prayer:* I note in my journal the insights and feelings that have surfaced during my prayer.

you will be
my witnesses
to the ends of
the earth.

Acts 1:8

Appendix 1: Discernment—
Decision-making in the Spirit

INTRODUCTION: DISCERNMENT OF SPIRITS

All of us have within us many feelings, promptings, and desires. At times we are thrown into confusion as we try to sort out things, especially when faced with the need to make a decision.

A continuing dialogue erupts within:

"What is best?"	"This is a good idea."
"It's never been done before."	"I can do that."
"What if I fail?"	"I think God wants this for me."
"Will I make money, become famous?"	"I'd enjoy that."
"That's selfish."	"I'm afraid."

This type of a dialogue can become paralyzing. How can we find our way through the maze to arrive at a decision that is authentically in harmony with the Spirit? How can we tell if the promptings we experience within ourselves are of the Spirit of Christ or if they receive their impetus from a spirit of darkness and evil? It is not always easy to tell the difference.

The spirit of goodness may not be attractive to us as it may entail self-sacrifice calling for radical trust. On the other hand, the dark spirit frequently presents itself in the guise of light. Prayerful discernment of the movements of the Spirit within ourselves is an essential prerequisite for growth and wholeness. As one progressively lives more in the Spirit, this discernment of spirits becomes not only more important but decidedly more difficult. Initially, choices were black and white, but they become much more refined; they become not so much a question of good or evil as a question of the greater or the lesser good.

Saint Ignatius challenges those who have chosen Christ to find God in all things. To help us to consistently do this, he offers an exercise of prayer and deliberation called the discernment of spirits. It is one of the most striking contributions of Saint Ignatius and holds, in miniature, the conversion dynamic of the total plan of the Exercises.

To habitually bring ourselves to the exercise of discernment is to consciously shape our life according to God's deepest desire and love for us. In the times of major decision-making, the discernment of spirits is an extremely effective tool.

PROCESS: DECISION-MAKING THROUGH DISCERNMENT

Preparation

God is love,
and whoever remains in love remains in God
and God in him [or her].

(1 John 4:16)

Loving God, you call me to goodness. May I always be aware that you have been present in my history and continue to be active in the events of my life.

Be with me now as I endeavor to discover your wish and intent for me: _____
_____ (clarify the decision to be made).

I beg that in this moment of decision I will be released from the obstacles, attachments, or dependencies that would serve to block or deflect this process of decision-making.

Prayer

God is light.
(1 John 1:5)

Loving God, open my heart that I may listen to the direction of your Spirit within me. May I be open to any manner in which you choose to speak to me. In this decision, may I be attentive to the events, the people, the memories, and the feelings that may be the means of your guidance. Free me, O God, to accept whatever decision will be most Christlike, most selfless in the service of others.

Spirit of God, grant me wisdom to hear and light to see.

Gathering the Evidence

Something . . .
which we have heard,
which we have seen with our own eyes,
which we have watched
and touched with our hands,
the Word of life—
this is our theme.

(1 John 1:1)

Loving God, bring me to a deeper awareness of the data and evidence I need in this process of decision-making.

Grant that I may be totally honest in posing to myself pertinent questions and open to hear and to see any information that may be relevant.

Possible questions:

- Where did this idea originate, and what prompted it?
- What concrete facts do I need to know to make an authentic decision (e.g., personal and financial cost, location, history and track record, risk or predictability, future potential, number of people involved, social implications, feelings involved)?
- How does this impending decision fit in with the pattern of God's action in my life, in my present commitments and state of life?

Focus

Our love must be not just words or mere talk,
but something active and genuine.
This will be the proof that we belong to the truth.

(1 John 3:18–19)

Loving God, make known to me the issues underlying this decision. Grant me the courage to look within and to dare to rate the issues in order of priority.

May I be blessed with clarity of truth to see within the decision at large your deepest call to me: _____ (clarify the underlying, key issue involved in this decision).

Prayerful Reflection: Inordinate Attachments

Be on your guard against false gods.
(1 John 5:20)

Loving God, lead me into an increased awareness of anything that may be blocking my freedom in this decision-making process. Make clear to me whatever attachments and dependencies possess and deflect me from your desire for me.

All-wise God, grant me the strength to desire the desire to be directed in all my life's decisions by you alone.

Considerations: How many excessive attachments are present in me, and how could they potentially affect this decision?

- Does the possibility of separation from family, friends, social situations tend to motivate my decision?
- Am I unduly attached to a particular home, church, location?
- Am I reluctant to sacrifice my own comfort; if so, to what degree?
- Is overconcern for success, achievement, prestige affecting my decision?
- How large a factor are excessive emotions in influencing this decision (e.g., fear, anger, enthusiasm)?

Prayerful Reflection: Test the Spirit

Not every spirit is to be trusted,
but test the spirits to see whether they are from God.
(1 John 4:1)

Creator God, be present to me as I list and weigh the advantages and disadvantages involved in the alternatives that are before me as I make this decision.

Alternative A		Alternative B	
Advantages	Disadvantages	Advantages	Disadvantages

Loving God, sensitize me to your presence as I experience you leading me in this decision-making process. Heighten my awareness to the feelings of consolation and desolation that serve to make known your desire for me.

May I recognize in the feelings of harmony, peace, and contentment your consolation drawing me. May I be responsive to your presence in the energizing, encouraging inspiration that accompanies your consolation.

At the same time, my God, I beg for a keen perception with which to recognize the signs of desolation that reveal to me the alternative that is contrary to your wish. In the desolation feelings of fear, anxiety, heaviness, restlessness, "puffed-up" inflation, discouragement, alienation, dryness, and lack of fervor, may I experience your firm and persistent hand guiding me away from what is not to my best interest and not in accordance with your plan for me.

Holy God, recall to me a former time of decision when I experienced your presence guiding me in the movements of consolation and desolation. Allow the grace of that time to be present now.

Spirit of God, be present in these movements leading to decision.

Direction: Test the Spirit.

In order to be sensitized to God's particular manner of acting in your life, recall a former time of discernment with its accompanying movements of consolation and desolation.

Consider separately each of the alternatives that are before you in the present discernment. Imaginatively create a scenario in which you adopt each alternative. Be aware of the movements of feelings that accompany each alternative. It will be helpful, and it may be necessary, to spend a day or longer with each scenario to better grasp the inner movement of the Spirit and the direction of the decision-making.

Election

The anointing
he gave you . . .
is true.
     (1 John 2:27)

Creator God, it is with a sincere heart that I decide: _____ (state alternative chosen). I give you thanks for your presence to me in this process of decision-making. I am grateful to you for the gifts of patience and perseverance that have sustained me along the way. Thank you, too, God, for the truth, the insight, and the clarity that I have received during this time of discernment.

Confirmation

And this is the proof that he remains in us:
the Spirit that he has given us.
$$\text{(1 John 3:24)}$$

Ever-faithful God, resting in my decision, I wait, trusting that if my decision is of the Spirit, you will show by external and internal means your confirmation.

I pray for a willingness to repeat the process of discernment if I do not receive confirmation.

Consideration:

Internal confirmation is seen in the sustained feelings of consolation: peace, freedom from anxiety, and so on.

External confirmation is recognized in a serene fitting together of circumstances, state of life, and other personal and communal commitments.

Conclusion

Holy God, I rejoice in your faithful love that continues within the events and circumstances of my life to draw me into an integration and harmony within myself, with the universe, and with you. Amen.

Appendix 2: Additional Prayers

Soul of Christ

Jesus, may all that is you flow into me.
May your body and blood be my food and drink.
May your passion and death be my strength and life.
Jesus, with you by my side enough has been given.
May the shelter I seek be the shadow of your cross.
Let me not run from the love which you offer,
>   but hold me safe from the forces of evil.
On each of my dyings shed your light and your love.
Keep calling to me until that day comes,
>   when with your saints, I may praise you forever.

(43, p. 3)

Letting Go

To a dear one about whom I have been concerned.
　　I behold the Christ in you.
　　I place you lovingly in the care of the Father.
　　I release you from my anxiety and concern.
　　I let go of my possessive hold on you.
　　I am willing to free you to follow the dictates
　　　　of your indwelling Lord.
　　I am willing to free you to live your life
　　　　according to your best light and understanding.
　　Husband, wife, child, friend—
　　I no longer try to force my ideas on you, my ways on you.
　　I lift my thoughts above you, above the personal level.
　　I see you as God sees you, a spiritual being, created
　　　　in His image, and endowed with qualities and abilities
　　　　that make you needed, and important—not only to me but
　　　　to God and His larger plan.
　　I do not bind you, I no longer believe that you do not have
　　　　the understanding you need in order to meet life.
　　I bless you,
　　　　I have faith in you,
　　　　　　I behold Jesus in you.

(Author unknown; 109, p. 100)

Prayer of Hope for the World

Lord God, we come to you in our need; create in us an awareness of the massive and seemingly irreversible proportions of the crisis we face today and a sense of urgency to activate the forces of goodness.

Where there is blatant nationalism, let there be a global, universal concern;
Where there is war and armed conflict, let there be negotiation;
Where there is stockpiling, let there be disarmament;
Where people struggle toward liberation, let there be noninterference;
Where there is consumerism, let there be a care to preserve the earth's resources;
Where there is abundance, let there be a choice for a simple lifestyle and sharing;
Where there is reliance on external activism, let there be a balance of prayerful dependence on you, O Lord;
Where there is selfish individualism, let there be an openness to community;
Where there is the sin of injustice, let there be guilt, confession, and atonement;
Where there is paralysis and numbness before the enormity of the problems, let there be confidence in our collective effort.

Lord, let us not so much be concerned to be cared for as to care, not so much to be materially secure as to know that we are loved by you. Let us not look to be served, but to place ourselves at the service of others whatever cost to self-interest, for it is in loving vulnerability that we, like Jesus, experience the fullness of what it means to be human. And it is in serving that we discover the healing springs of life that will bring about a new birth to our earth and hope to our world. Amen. (14, pp. 7–8)

Appendix 3: For Spiritual Directors

The passages and commentaries in this guide are keyed to the Spiritual Exercises of Saint Ignatius. The numbers in parentheses indicate the numbered paragraphs or sections as found in the original text of the Exercises.

For "The Principle and Foundation," see *Love* of the Take and Receive series. For Week 1, See *Forgiveness*; for Week 2, see *Birth*; and for Week 3, see *Surrender*.

Appendix 4: List of Approaches to Prayer

Index of Scriptural Passages

The passages in this index are keyed to volumes in the Take and Receive series: *L* refers to *Love*, *F* to *Forgiveness*, *B* to *Birth*, *S* to *Surrender*, and *FR* to *Freedom*.

151

Bibliography

1. Abbott, Walter M., ed. *The Documents of Vatican II.* New York: American Press, 1966.
2. Albright, W. F., and C. S. Mann. *Matthew.* Garden City, NY: Doubleday and Co., 1971.
3. Barclay, William. *The Acts of the Apostles.* Philadelphia: Westminster Press, 1976.
4. _____. *The Gospel of John.* 2 vols. Philadelphia: Westminster Press, 1975.
5. _____. *The Gospel of Luke.* Philadelphia: Westminster Press, 1975.
6. _____. *The Gospel of Mark.* Philadelphia: Westminster Press, 1975.
7. _____. *The Gospel of Matthew.* 2 vols. Philadelphia: Westminster Press, 1975.
8. _____. *The Letters of John and Jude.* Philadelphia: Westminster Press, 1976.
9. _____. *The Letters to the Corinthians.* Philadelphia: Westminster Press, 1975.
10. _____. *The Letters to the Philippians, Colossians, and Thessalonians.* Philadelphia: Westminster Press, 1975.
11. _____. *The Revelation of John.* 2 vols. Philadelphia: Westminster Press, 1976.
12. Barti, Markus. *Ephesians 1–3.* Garden City, NY: Doubleday and Co., 1974.
13. Benoit, Pierre. *The Passion and Resurrection of Jesus Christ.* New York: Herder and Herder, 1969.
14. Bergan, Jacqueline, and Marie Schwan. *Peace.* 1983. Available through the Center for Christian Renewal, Box 87, Crookston, MN 56716.
15. Bridges, Robert, ed. *Poems of Gerard Manley Hopkins.* New York: Oxford University Press, 1948.
16. Brown, Raymond. *The Birth of the Messiah.* Garden City, NY: Doubleday and Co., 1979.
17. _____. *The Epistles of John.* Garden City, NY: Doubleday and Co., 1982.
18. _____. *The Gospel According to John.* 2 vols. Garden City, NY: Doubleday and Co., 1966.

19. _____. *The Gospel According to John*. 2 vols. Garden City, NY: Double-day and Co., 1966.
20. _____. *The Jerome Biblical Commentary*. Englewood Cliffs, NJ: Prentice-Hall, 1968.
21. _____. *The Virginal Conception and Bodily Resurrection of Jesus*. New York: Paulist Press, 1973.
22. Brueggemann, Walter. *The Prophetic Imagination*. Philadelphia: Fortress Press, 1978.
23. Caird, G. B. *Saint Luke*. London: Penguin Books, 1963.
24. Capra, Fritjof. *The Turning Point*. New York: Simon and Schuster, 1982.
25. Claudel, Paul. "The Tidings Brought to Mary" in vol. 3 of *A Treasury of the Theater*. New York: Simon and Schuster, 1982.
26. Clift, Jean Dalby, and Wallace B. Clift. *Symbols of Transformation in Dreams*. New York: Crossroad, 1986.
27. Clift, Wallace B. *Jung and Christianity*. New York: Crossroad, 1982.
28. Collins, Adela Yarbro. *The Apocalypse*. Wilmington, DE: Michael Glazier, 1979.
29. Cooper, J. C. *An Illustrated Encyclopaedia of Traditional Symbols*. London: Thames and Hudson, 1978.
30. *Encyclopaedia Britannica*, s. v. "coronation."
31. Cowan, Marian, and John C. Futrell. *The Spiritual Exercises of St. Ignatius of Loyola: A Handbook for Directors*. New York: Le Jacq Publishing, 1982.
32. Crossman, Dominic M. "The Gospel of Jesus Christ." Stonebridge Priory, Lake Bluff, IL, 1963. Mimeographed notes.
33. Crowe, Jerome. *The Acts*. Wilmington, DE: Michael Glazier, 1979.
34. cummings, e. e. *No Thanks*. New York: Golden Eagle Press, 1935.
35. De Grazia, Ted. *The Yaqui Easter*. Tucson, AZ: University of Arizona Press, 1968.
36. de Mello, Anthony. *Sadhana: A Way to God*. Saint Louis: Institute of Jesuit Sources, 1978.
37. English, John. *Choosing Life*. New York: Paulist Press, 1978.

38. _____. *Spiritual Freedom*. Guelph, Ontario: Loyola House, 1974.
39. Fallon, Francis T. *2 Corinthians*. Wilmington, DE: Michael Glazier, 1980.
40. Faricy, Robert. *The Spirituality of Teilhard de Chardin*. Minneapolis: Winston Press, 1981.
41. Fenton, J. C. *Saint Matthew*. London: Penguin Books, 1963.
42. Fitzmeyer, Joseph. *The Gospel According to Luke X—XXIV*. Garden City, NY: Doubleday and Co., 1985.
43. Fleming, David. *The Spiritual Exercises: Literal Translation and a Contemporary Reading*. Saint Louis: Institute of Jesuit Sources, 1978.
44. Ford, J. Massyngberde. *Revelation*. Garden City, NY: Doubleday and Co., 1975.
45. Fox, Matthew. *Breakthrough*. Garden City, NY: Image Books, 1977.
46. Getty, Mary Ann. *Philippians and Philemon*. Wilmington, DE: Michael Glazier, 1980.
47. Gore, Rick. "The Once and Future Universe." *National Geographic* 163 (June 1983): 704–749.
48. Hall, Nor. *The Moon and the Virgin*. New York: Harper and Row, 1980.
49. Harrington, Wilfred. *Mark*. Wilmington, DE: Michael Glazier, 1979.
50. Houselander, Caryll. *The Risen Christ*. New York: Sheed and Ward, 1958.
51. Jensen, Joseph. *Isaiah 1–39*. Wilmington, DE: Michael Glazier, 1984.
52. Johnson, Robert A. *She*. New York: Harper and Row, 1977.
53. Jung, Carl G. *Aion*. Princeton, NJ: Princeton University Press, 1959.
54. _____. *Four Archetypes*. Princeton, NJ: Princeton University Press, 1959.
55. _____. *Man and His Symbols*. New York: Valor Publications, 1964.
56. Kelsey, Morton. *Resurrection: Release from Oppression*. New York: Paulist Press, 1985.
57. Küng, Hans. *On Being a Christian*. Garden City, NY: Doubleday and Co., 1976.
58. Lacey, Robert. *Majesty*. New York: Harcourt Brace Jovanovich, 1977.
59. La Verdiere, Eugene. *Luke*. Wilmington, DE: Michael Glazier, 1980.
60. Leonard, Linda Schierse. *On the Way to the Wedding*. Boston: Shambhala, 1986.

61. Luke, Helen M. *Woman: Earth and Spirit.* New York: Crossroads, 1985.

62. McBrien, Richard P. *Catholicism.* 2 vols. Minneapolis: Winston Press, 1980.

63. McClain, Jane C. "Beginning with the Goddess." *Creation* 1 (January–February 1986): 26–27.

64. McGann, Diarmuid. *The Journeying Self.* New York: Paulist Press, 1985.

65. McKenzie, John. *Dictionary of the Bible.* Milwaukee: Bruce Publishing Co., 1965.

66. _____. *Second Isaiah.* Garden City, NY: Doubleday and Co., 1968.

67. McPolin, James. *John.* Wilmington, DE: Michael Glazier, 1979.

68. Magana, Jose. *A Strategy for Liberation.* Hicksville, NY: Exposition Press, 1974.

69. Maloney, George. *Mary, the Womb of God.* Denville, NJ: Dimension Books, 1976.

70. _____. *Singers of the New Song.* Notre Dame, IN: Ave Maria Press, 1985.

71. _____. *The First Day of Eternity; Resurrection Now.* New York: Crossroads, 1982.

72. Marsh, John. *St. John.* London: Penguin Books, 1968.

73. Meier, John P. *Matthew.* Wilmington, DE: Michael Glazier, 1980.

74. Mondadori, Arnoldo, ed. *Dante: His Life, His Times, His Works.* New York: American Heritage Press, 1968.

75. Moore, Sabastian. *The Inner Loneliness.* New York: Crossroads, 1982.

76. Morton, H. V. "In the London of the New Queen." *National Geographic* 104 (September 1953): 291–342.

77. Munck, Johannes. *The Acts of the Apostles.* Garden City, NY: Doubleday and Co., 1967.

78. Murphy, Roland. *Seven Books of Wisdom.* Milwaukee: Bruce Publishing Co., 1960.

79. Murphy-O'Connor, Jerome. *1 Corinthians.* Wilmington, DE: Michael Glazier, 1979.

80. National Conference of Catholic Bishops. *The Sacramentary.* New York: Catholic Books Publishing Co., 1974.

81. Neumann, Erick. *The Great Mother.* Princeton, NJ: Princeton University Press, 1963.

82. Nineham, D. E. *Mark*. Baltimore: Penguin Books, 1963.
83. Orr, William F., and James Arthur Walther. *1 Corinthians*. Garden City, NY: Doubleday and Co., 1976.
84. Osiek, Carolyn. *Galatians*. Wilmington, DE: Michael Glazier, 1980.
85. Paoli, Arturo. *Freedom to Be Free*. Maryknoll, NY: Orbis Books, 1973.
86. Pennington, Basil. *Centering Prayer*. Garden City, NY: Image Books, 1982.
87. Perkins, Pheme. *Resurrection*. Garden City, NY: Doubleday and Co., 1984.
88. _____. *The Johannine Epistles*. Wilmington, DE: Michael Glazier, 1979.
89. Pope, Marvin H. *Song of Songs*. Garden City, NY: Doubleday and Co., 1977.
90. Rahner, Karl. *Spiritual Exercises*. New York: Herder and Herder, 1956.
91. Reese, M. James. *The Book of Wisdom; Song of Songs*. Wilmington, DE: Michael Glazier, 1983.
92. Robbins, Anthony. *Unlimited Power*. New York: Simon and Schuster, 1986.
93. Rosenblatt, Roger. "A Letter to the Year 2086." *Time* 128 (29 December 1986): 24–29.
94. Roustang, Francois. *Growth in the Spirit*. New York: Sheed and Ward, 1966.
95. Sanford, Agnes. *Creation Waits*. Plainfield, NJ: Logos International, 1978.
96. Sanford, John. *Healing and Wholeness*. New York: Paulist Press, 1977.
97. _____. *The Kingdom Within*. New York: Paulist Press, 1970.
98. Schaef, Anne Wilson. *Co-Dependence*. Minneapolis: Winston Press, 1986.
99. Schauss, Hayyim. *The Jewish Festivals*. New York: Union of American Hebrew Congregations, 1938.
100. Schillebeeckx, Edward. *Jesus: An Experiment in Christology*. New York: Crossroads, 1981.
101. Scullion, John. *Isaiah 40–66*. Wilmington, DE: Michael Glazier, 1982.
102. Stanley, David M. *A Modern Scriptural Approach to the Spiritual Exercises*. Saint Louis: Institute of Jesuit Sources, 1971.
103. _____. *I Encountered God*. Saint Louis: Institute of Jesuit Sources, 1986.
104. Swain, Lionel. *Ephesians*. Wilmington, DE: Michael Glazier, 1980.

105. Tannehill, Robert C. *A Mirror for Disciples: A Study of the Gospel of Mark.* Nashville, TN: Disciples Resources, 1977.

106. Taylor, Vincent. *The Gospel According to St. Mark.* New York: Saint Martin's Press, 1966.

107. Thurian, Max. *Mary, Mother of All Christians.* New York: Herder and Herder, 1964.

108. Vann, Gerald. *The Pain of Christ.* Springfield, IL: Templegate, 1947.

109. Veltri, John. *Orientations.* Vol. 1, *A Collection of Helps for Prayer.* Guelph, Ontario: Loyola House, 1979.

110. _____. *Orientations.* Vol. 2, *Annotation 19: Tentative Edition.* Guelph, Ontario: Loyola House, 1981.

111. Wilder, Thornton. *Our Town. A Treasury of the Theater.* Vol. 3, New York: Simon and Schuster, 1963.

Acknowledgments (*continued*)

The excerpt on page 66 is from *Dante: His Life, His Times, His Works* created by the editors of Arnoldo Mondadori Editore, translated from the Italian by Giuseppina T. Salvadori and Bernice L. Lewis, anthology by Prof. Thomas G. Bergin. Copyright © 1968 by Arnoldo Mondadori-Milano. Published in 1970 by American Heritage Press, New York.

The excerpt on page 68 is from *Four Archetypes: Mother, Rebirth, Spirit, Trickster*, trans. R. F. C. Hull. From *The Collected Works of C. G. Jung*, vol. 9, part 1, Bollingen Series XX. Copyright © 1959, 1969 by Princeton University Press. Reprinted with permission of Princeton University Press.

The excerpt on pages 84 to 85 is from *The Pain of Christ* by Gerald Vann (Springfield, IL: Templegate, 1947). Used with permission.

The selection on page 97 from *Spiritual Exercises: Literal Translation and a Contemporary Reading* by David L. Fleming, SJ (The Institute of Jesuit Sources, St. Louis, 1978), is used with permission.

"love is a place" on page 113 is reprinted from NO THANKS by e. e. cummings by permission of Liveright Publishing Corporation. Copyright 1935 by e. e. cummings. Copyright © 1968 by Marion Morehouse Cummings. Copyright © 1973, 1978 by the Trustees for the e. e. cummings Trust. Copyright © 1973, 1978 by George James Firmage.

The selection on page 143 is from *Orientations, Volume 1: A Collection of Helps for Prayer* by John Veltri (Guelph, Ontario: Loyola House, 1979). Used with permission.

The Magnificat on page 21 is from *Psalms Anew in Inclusive Language* by Nancy Schreck, OSF, and Maureen Leach, OSF. Copyright © 1986 by Saint Mary's Press. Used with permission.

To Our Readers:

It would be helpful to us, as we prepare to write the subsequent volumes of this series of guides for prayer, if you would be willing to respond to the following questions, and send your response to us.

   Thank You.

   Jacqueline
   Marie

———————————————————————————————————————

Please check the appropriate answers and add your comments.

1. I used the guide for prayer
   _____ regularly over a period of _____ (weeks or months).
   _____ irregularly.
   Comment:

2. I found the format (i.e., cover design, paper, type, layout)
   _____ helpful to my prayer.
   _____ unhelpful to my prayer.
   Comment:

3. I found the commentaries
   _____ helpful for entering into prayer.
   _____ difficult to understand.
   Comment:

4. The commentaries that were most helpful were on pages _____
   _____

5. I (used or did not use) the approaches to prayer.
   Comment:

6. What I liked best about the guide for prayer is _____
   _____

7. The following changes or additions would make the guide for prayer more helpful: _____

_____
(Signature optional)

Mail to Center for Christian Renewal at Jesuit Retreat House, 4800 Fahrnwald Road, Oshkosh, WI 54901.